POLITICS UK

The UK Cabinet Manual

A guide to laws, conventions and rules on the operation of government

Contents

Introduction

Chapter One: The Sovereign

Chapter Two: Elections and government formation

Chapter Three: The Executive – the Prime Minister, ministers and the structure of government

Chapter Four: Collective Cabinet decision-making

Chapter Five: The Executive and Parliament

Chapter Six: The Executive and the law

Chapter Seven: Ministers and the Civil Service

Chapter Eight: Relations with the Devolved Administrations and local government Devolution

Introduction

Parliamentary democracy

1. The UK is a parliamentary democracy which has a constitutional sovereign as Head of State; a sovereign Parliament, which is supreme to all other government institutions, consisting of the Sovereign, the House of Commons and the House of Lords, an Executive drawn from and accountable to Parliament, and an independent judiciary.

2. Constitutional convention is that executive power is exercised by the Sovereign's Government, which has a democratic mandate to govern. Members of the Government are normally members of the House of Commons or the House of Lords and the Government is directly accountable to Parliament. The government of the day holds office by virtue of its ability to command the confidence of the House of Commons. Elections are held at least every five years to ensure broad and continued accountability to the people. Election candidates usually represent political parties, and party numbers in the House of Commons determine the composition of the Government.

3. Parliament is sovereign and it has provided by Acts of Parliament –which, by their nature, may be repealed – for certain issues to be considered and determined at different levels: within the EU; by the Devolved Administrations; and by local government.

The UK constitution

4. The UK does not have a codified constitution. There is no single document that describes, establishes or regulates the structures of the state and the way in which these relate to the people. Instead, the constitutional order has evolved over time and continues to do so. It consists of various institutions, statutes, judicial decisions, principles and practices that are commonly understood as „constitutional". The UK does not have a constitutional court to rule on the implications of a codified constitution, and the sovereignty of Parliament is therefore unrestrained by such a court.

5. Constitutional matters and practices may include: statutes, such as the Magna Carta in 1215; the Bill of Rights and Scottish Claim of Right Act in 1689; the Acts of Union; the various Acts extending the voting franchise; the Parliament Acts in 1911 and 1949 limiting the powers of the House of Lords; the European Communities Act 1972; the Northern Ireland Act 1998, the Scotland Act 1998; and the

Government of Wales Acts of 1998 and 2006 the Royal Prerogative, which is the residual power inherent in the Sovereign, and now exercised mostly on the advice of the

Prime Minister and Ministers of the Crown judicial decisions, made by the Supreme Court (formerly the House of Lords), the Court of Appeal and the High Court (in England, Wales and Northern Ireland) and the Court of Session in Scotland conventions, rules of constitutional practice that are regarded as binding in operation but not in law European and international law, both of which inform and influence the UK"s constitution.

The Sovereign

6. The Sovereign is the Head of State of the UK, providing stability, continuity and a national focus. By convention, the Sovereign does not become publicly involved in the party politics of government, although he or she is entitled to be informed and consulted, and to advise, encourage and warn ministers. For this reason, there is a convention of confidentiality surrounding the Sovereign"s communications with his other ministers. The Sovereign retains prerogative powers but, by constitutional convention, the majority of these powers are exercised by, or on the advice of, his or her responsible ministers, save in a few exceptional instances, (the „reserve powers"). Paragraphs 58 and 59 of Chapter 2 are examples of the Sovereign"s reserve powers.

Parliament

7. Parliament has a number of functions, which include controlling national expenditure and taxation; making law; scrutinising executive action; being the source from which the Government is drawn; and debating the issues of the day. All areas of the UK are represented in Parliament and it provides a forum for Members of Parliament (MPs) to speak and correspond on behalf of their constituents, where they can seek redress if necessary.

8. Parliament comprises the Sovereign in Parliament and two Houses: the House of Commons, which is wholly elected, and the House of Lords, which comprises the Lords Spiritual and Temporal. Parliament has overall control of the public purse; the Government may not levy taxes, raise loans or spend public money unless and until it has authorisation from Parliament.

9. In the exercise of its legislative powers, Parliament is sovereign. In practice, however, Parliament has chosen to be constrained in various ways – for example by its commitment to the rule of law, through its Acts, and elements of European and other international law.

10. Parliament also scrutinises executive action. Indeed, the government of the day is primarily responsible to Parliament for its day-to-day actions. This function is exercised through a variety of

mechanisms, such as the select committee system, parliamentary questions, oral and written statements and debates in both Houses.

11. By the Scotland Act 1998, the Government of Wales Acts 1998 and 2006, and the Northern Ireland Act 1998, Parliament devolved powers over areas of domestic policy such as housing, health and education to directly elected legislatures in Scotland, Wales and Northern Ireland.

Parliament retains the legal power to continue to legislate on these matters, but it does not normally do so without the consent of these devolved legislatures.

The Prime Minister and ministers

12. Ministers act pursuant to statutory powers conferred on them by Parliament, to the Royal Prerogative and to inherent or "common law" powers. They are required to act in accordance with the law. The courts and other bodies have a role in ensuring that ministerial action is carried out lawfully.

13. The role of the Prime Minister and Cabinet are governed largely by convention. The Prime Minister is the Sovereign's chief adviser, chairs Cabinet and has overall responsibility for the organisation of government. Cabinet is the ultimate arbiter of all government policy; decisions made at Cabinet and Cabinet committee level are binding on all members of the Government, save where collective agreement is expressly set aside, and any minister who cannot accept them is expected to resign.

14. Ministers are individually responsible to Parliament for departmental matters and for their own conduct in office. They are collectively responsible to Parliament for the policies of the government to which they belong.

15. Ministers hold office as long as they have the confidence of the Prime Minister. They are supported by civil servants, non-partisan servants of the Crown. Civil servants are required to act with honesty, objectivity, impartiality and integrity. In return, ministers are expected to ensure that they do not bring the impartiality of the Civil Service into question, or draw the Civil Service into conflict with the Civil Service Code or the requirements of the Constitutional Reform and Governance Act 2010.

The judiciary

16. The judiciary interprets and applies the law in its decisions. It is a long-established constitutional principle that the judiciary is independent of both the government of the day and Parliament so as to ensure the even-handed administration of justice. Civil servants, ministers, and in particular the Lord Chancellor, are under a duty to uphold the continued independence of the judiciary, and must not seek to influence particular judicial decisions. The Lord Chief Justice is the head of the judiciary in

England and Wales. The Lord President of the Court of Session and the Lord Chief Justice of Northern Ireland are the heads of the judiciary in Scotland and Northern Ireland respectively. The Supreme Court is the final court of appeal for all civil cases in the UK and for all criminal cases in England, Wales and Northern Ireland.

European Union and other international law

17. Parliament has provided for the incorporation of the EU into the UK"s domestic law through the European Communities Act 1972 and by Acts of Parliament.

18. The UK has also ratified a wide range of other treaties that form part of the constitutional framework – for example the Charter of the United Nations, the North Atlantic Treaty and the various agreements of the World Trade Organization.

Chapter One

The UK is a constitutional monarchy. The Sovereign has a number of ceremonial and constitutional duties in relation to the Government. The Sovereign is the Head of State, the Head of the Armed Forces, the Supreme Governor of the Church of England and the fount of honour. The Sovereign appoints the Prime Minister and other ministers, and many of the Government's powers derive from those of the Sovereign. The Government is thus 'the Sovereign's Government' as well as commanding the confidence of the House of Commons.

This chapter covers:

- Ceremonial and constitutional duties
- The Royal Prerogative
- Succession and coronation
- Absence and incapacity of the Sovereign
- The Privy Council
- The Established Church.

The Sovereign

Ceremonial and constitutional duties

1.1   The Sovereign fulfils a number of ceremonial and constitutional duties relevant to the Government. The Sovereign appoints the Prime Minister and, on his or her advice, other ministers (see Chapter Three). The Sovereign opens each new session of Parliament,2 and brings the session to an end, proroguing Parliament if necessary by Order in Council. Under the Fixed-term Parliaments Act 2011, Parliament is dissolved automatically 17 working days before the fixed date for the election.3 Where in accordance with the Act there is to be an early election, the Sovereign fixes the date of the election by Proclamation on the recommendation of the Prime Minister.4 The Sovereign in all cases fixes by Proclamation the date for the next meeting of Parliament. A bill which has completed all of its prior Parliamentary stages becomes law when Royal Assent (the formal approval of the Sovereign) is given.5 The Sovereign also appoints the First Minister of Scotland and the First Minister for Wales, and has a role in relation to the Devolved Administrations, as set out in legislation.6

1.2   The Sovereign is Head of the Armed Forces. Armed Forces recruits are required to swear an oath of allegiance to the Sovereign (or make a solemn affirmation to the same effect).7 All titles of honour (for example knighthoods) are conferred by the Sovereign, mostly on the advice of the government of the day, although there are some honours that the Sovereign confers at his or her own discretion. An example would be an Order of Merit. British honours are usually conferred by the Sovereign on the advice of the Cabinet Office, while the Foreign and Commonwealth Office (FCO) advises the Sovereign where honorary decorations and awards are granted to people from other countries.8

1.3   As Head of State, the Sovereign undertakes and hosts a number of state visits, helping to build relations with other nations. In addition to the UK, the Sovereign is Head of State of a number of other Commonwealth realms.9 Her Majesty the Queen is also Head of the Commonwealth,10 a voluntary association of 54 countries.

1.4   The Sovereign has a role in relation to the Channel Islands and the Isle of Man, which are not part of the UK but are self-governing Crown Dependencies.11 The Sovereign is ultimately responsible for the good government of the Crown Dependencies and the Lieutenant

Governors are his or her personal representatives. Constitutionally, the UK is responsible for their defence and representation internationally. The Crown Dependencies make annual voluntary contributions towards the costs of their defence and international representation by the UK. The Privy Counsellor with responsibility for the Crown Dependencies is currently the Lord Chancellor. There are also 14 Overseas Territories12 for which the UK is responsible. They are not constitutionally part of the UK, but the Sovereign has responsibility for appointing a Governor or Commissioner to represent him or her in the Overseas Territory.

The Royal Prerogative

1.5   The scope of the Royal Prerogative power, which is the residual power inherent in the Sovereign, has evolved over time.13 Originally the Royal Prerogative would only have been exercised by the reigning Sovereign. However, ministers now exercise the bulk of the prerogative powers, either in their own right or through the advice that they provide to the Sovereign, which he or she is constitutionally bound to follow. The Sovereign is, however, entitled to be informed and consulted, and to advise, encourage and warn ministers. More detail on the exercise of the Royal Prerogative by ministers can be found in Chapter Three.

Succession and coronation

1.6   The succession to the Crown is automatic; on the death of the previous Sovereign the heir succeeds without any further ceremony and, as in the case of Edward VIII, can reign without ever being formally crowned.14 The coronation ceremony usually takes place some months later.

1.7   At the first Privy Council following accession, the Sovereign is required to take an oath to maintain and preserve the Presbyterian Church of Scotland.15 Subsequently, at the first Parliament of the reign,16 the Sovereign is required to declare that they are a faithful Protestant and will secure the Protestant succession.17 (See paragraphs 1.20 and 1.21 on the Established Church.) Under the Coronation Oath, the Sovereign swears by oath to govern the people of the UK and the Commonwealth realms according to their agreed laws and customs; to cause law and justice, in mercy, to be executed in all judgements; to the utmost of his or her power maintain the laws of God, the true profession of the Gospel and in the United Kingdom the Protestant Reformed Religion established by law; and to preserve to the bishops and clergy of England and to the churches committed to their charge all the rights and privileges which the law accords.18

Absence and incapacity of the Sovereign

1.8 When the Sovereign is absent from the country for a short period or temporarily incapacitated or for some definite cause not available, his or her functions are delegated to Counsellors of State.19 These are currently the Sovereign's spouse and the four nearest in line to the Throne. Two or more Counsellors of State may exercise any of the functions of the Sovereign except the powers to grant any rank, title or dignity of the peerage, or to signify Royal Assent to any amendment to the Act of Settlement 1700 or Royal Style and Titles.

1.9 When the Sovereign is incapacitated for a longer period, or is under the age of 18, a Regent may be appointed.20 With regard to incapacity of the Sovereign, a Regency can only be declared if three or more of the wife or husband of the Sovereign, the Lord Chancellor, the Speaker of the House of Commons, the Lord Chief Justice of England and Wales, and the Master of the Rolls determine that it is necessary because of the bodily or mental infirmity of the Sovereign. A Regent must take the oaths of the Sovereign, except the Coronation Oath, and may exercise any of the powers of the Sovereign, except assent to any bill for changing the order of succession to the Crown as defined by the Act of Settlement 1700 or for repealing or altering the Act preserving the Presbyterian system of Church government in Scotland.

The Privy Council

1.10 The Privy Council21 advises the Sovereign on the exercise of the prerogative powers and certain functions assigned to the Sovereign and the Council by Act of Parliament. The Privy Council is established under the Royal Prerogative and is the mechanism through which interdepartmental agreement is reached on those items of government business which, for historical or other reasons, fall to ministers as Privy Counsellors rather than as departmental ministers. For example, certain Statutory Instruments must take the form of Orders in Council.

1.11 Those appointed to the Privy Council mostly comprise ministers, other Parliamentarians and members of the judiciary. The appointment of Privy Counsellors is made by the Sovereign on the recommendation of the Prime Minister. Appointment to the Privy Council is for life and therefore the majority of Counsellors play no part in the Privy Council's day-to-day business, which is largely conducted by ministers of the government of the day.

1.12 Exceptionally, non-Cabinet ministers attending Cabinet and senior members of opposition parties can be given briefings on confidential terms ('Privy Council terms'). Such an arrangement is entirely voluntary, and anyone not wishing to be briefed on such terms may decline the invitation. Having accepted a briefing on Privy Counsellor terms, he or she is understood to have agreed to treat it as confidential.

1.13 The Lord President of the Council (fourth of the Great Officers of State)22 is responsible for presiding over meetings of the Privy Council, which are held by the Sovereign, and also forms part of the quorum on matters approved 'by the Lords of the Privy Council'. The post is generally a Cabinet post and is often held by the Leader of either the House of Commons or the House of Lords. The post of Lord President is currently held by the Deputy Prime Minister.

Committees of the Privy Council

1.14 Cabinet is the executive committee of the Privy Council. There are a number of standing committees of the Privy Council (for example the Judicial Committee, which among other things is the court of final appeal for the UK Overseas Territories and Crown Dependencies, and for some Commonwealth countries).

Privy Council meetings

1.15 Council meetings are occasions on which the Sovereign conveys formal approval to Orders in Council. The quorum is three, and summonses go only to government ministers and are issued on a rota basis. Once a minister has accepted a summons to a meeting of the Privy Council, this takes precedence over all other engagements.23

1.16 Decisions of the Council are recorded in Orders. Orders in Council, which are made by Her Majesty in Council, are a form of primary or secondary legislation.

• An Order in Council made under the Royal Prerogative is regarded as a form of primary legislation. Examples of this are Orders for the Prorogation of Parliament, approving or rejecting petitions or legislation of the Crown Dependencies and Orders dealing with certain matters concerning the Overseas Territories.

• An Order in Council made under a power conferred by legislation will usually be subject to a Parliamentary procedure.

Examples of this are Orders giving effect to United Nations (UN) Measures or sanctions, and transfer of functions orders under the Ministers of the Crown Act 1975.

1.17 Orders of Council are Orders that do not require personal approval by the Sovereign, but which can be made by 'the Lords of the Privy Council' (that is, ministers). Again, these can be statutory or made under the Royal Prerogative. Whether statutory Orders are also Statutory Instruments depends on the wording of the particular Act under which they are made.

• Examples of statutory Orders of Council include approval of regulations made by the General Medical Council and other regulatory bodies.

• Examples of prerogative Orders of Council include approval of amendments to the by-laws of Chartered bodies (institutions such as the Royal Institution of Chartered Surveyors and the Royal British Legion).

1.18 Her Majesty in Council also gives approval to statutory Proclamations for new coinage and for certain bank holidays. Prerogative Proclamations for proroguing Parliament and setting the date of the meeting of a new Parliament are approved in Council, as are Proclamations under the Fixed-term Parliaments Act 2011 setting the date for an election which has been varied in accordance with the terms of that Act.

Committees of Privy Counsellors

1.19 In addition to the permanent standing committees of the Privy Council, committees of Privy Counsellors are occasionally formed on an ad hoc basis to undertake a particular task, and are then dissolved. These are wholly independent of the Privy Council Office and do not report to the Lord President. The Chair, membership and terms of reference of each committee are determined by ministers and vary according to the issue which the committee is considering. Examples include the Committees chaired by Lord Newton of Braintree[24] and by Lord Butler of Brockwell.[25]

The Established Church

1.20 The Sovereign is the Supreme Governor of the Church of England and must, under the provisions of the Act of Settlement 1700, join in communion with it.[26] The Church's legislation[27] forms part of the public law of England. The responsibility for initiating Church legislation rests with the Church's General Synod. Once approved by the General Synod, a draft measure requires approval by both Houses of Parliament and Royal Assent before becoming law. The Archbishops of Canterbury and York, the Bishops of London, Winchester and Durham and 21 further bishops are entitled ex oficio to sit in the House of Lords.[28]

1.21 The Church was disestablished in the whole of Ireland in 1871 and in Wales in 1920.[29] The Church of Scotland, which has a Presbyterian system of church government, is the national church in Scotland. The Church of Scotland Act 1921 guaranteed its spiritual independence.

Notes

1   Jack M (ed.) (2011) Erskine May's Treatise on the Law, Privileges, Proceedings and Usage of Parliament, 24th edition. London: LexisNexis Butterworths, pp. 158–161.

2   Ibid., pp. 144–145.

3   Fixed-term Parliaments Act 2011, s.3(1).

4   Ibid., s.2(7).

5   Jack (ed.) Erskine May, pp. 642–645.

6   See the Scotland Act 1998 and the Government of Wales Act 2006 for more information. Throughout this manual, reference is made to the 'Scottish Government' and the 'Welsh Government' although their statutory titles are 'Scottish Executive' and 'Welsh Assembly Government' (the Scotland Act 1998 and the Government of Wales Act 2006). These two organisations have made clear their preference to be known by these titles. The Government is legislating in the Scotland Bill to change the statutory title for the Scottish Executive to the Scottish Government. It is examining whether a suitable legislative vehicle can be found to change the statutory title for the Welsh Assembly Government to the Welsh Government.

7   Ministry of Defence (2011) Manual of Service Law, Chapter 18, paragraph 8.

8   For more information see: Directgov, 'The honours process explained': www.direct.gov.uk/en/Governmentcitizensandrights/ UKgovernment/Honoursawardsandmedals/ DG_067909.

9   They are Antigua and Barbuda, Australia, the Bahamas, Barbados, Belize, Canada, Grenada, Jamaica, New Zealand, Papua New Guinea, the Solomon Islands, St Christopher and Nevis, St Lucia, St Vincent and the Grenadines, and Tuvalu.

10 The Commonwealth (1949) London Declaration.

11 Ministry of Justice (2011) Background Briefing on the Crown Dependencies: Jersey, Guernsey and the Isle of Man.

12 They are Anguilla, Bermuda, British Antarctic Territory, the British Indian Ocean Territory, the British Virgin Islands, the Cayman Islands, the Falkland Islands, Gibraltar, Montserrat, the Pitcairn Group of Islands, St Helena, Ascension Island and Tristan da Cunha, South Georgia and the South Sandwich Islands, the Sovereign Base Areas of Akrotiri and Dhekelia on Cyprus, and Turks and Caicos Islands.

13 For more information on the Royal Prerogative, see: House of Commons Library (2009) The Royal Prerogative, Standard Note SN/PC/03861.

14   Act of Settlement 1700.

15   Act of Union 1707.

16 The modern practice is to take the oath at the first State Opening of Parliament of the new reign. Her Majesty the Queen took the oath on 4 November 1952.

17   Accession Declaration Act 1910.

18   The exact form of the Coronation Oath may vary but it is based on the Coronation Oath Act 1689. For more information, see: House of Commons Library (2008) The Coronation Oath, Standard Note SN/PC/00435.

19   Regency Acts 1937, 1943, 1953.

20   Regency Act 1937.

21   For more information, see: www.privycouncil.independent.gov.uk.

22   The Great Oficers of State for England and Wales comprise: Lord High Steward, Lord High Chancellor, Lord High Treasurer, Lord President of the Council, Lord Privy Seal, Lord Great Chamberlain, Lord High Constable, Earl Marshal and Lord High Admiral.

23   Cabinet Ofice (2010) Ministerial Code, paragraph 2.5.

24   See: Privy Counsellor Review Committee (2003) Anti-terrorism, Crime and Security Act 2001 Review: Report (HC381). London: The Stationery Ofice.

25   See: Report of a Committee of Privy Counsellors (2004) Review of Intelligence on Weapons of Mass Destruction (HC898). London: The Stationery Ofice.

26   Act of Settlement 1700, s.3.

27   For more information on Church of England measures, see: House of Commons Information Ofice (2010) Church of England Measures, Factsheet L10 and the Church of England Assembly (Powers) Act 1919.

28   Bishoprics Act 1878, s.5.

29   The Irish Church Act 1869 came into force in 1871. There were two Acts disestablishing the Church in Wales: the Welsh Church Act 1914 and the Welsh Church (Temporalities) Act 1919, both of which came into force in 1920.

Chapter Two

A government holds office by virtue of its ability to command the confidence of the House of Commons, chosen by the electorate in a general election.

This chapter covers:

- General elections
- Meeting of the new Parliament
- The principles of government formation
- Parliaments with an overall majority in the House of Commons
- Parliaments with no overall majority in the House of Commons
- Change of Prime Minister or government during a Parliament
- Pre-election contact with opposition parties
- Dissolution of Parliament
- finalisation of Parliamentary business
- Restrictions on government activity.

Elections and government formation

General elections

2.1   General elections allow voters on the electoral roll to cast their ballot for an MP to represent them in the House of Commons. In accordance with the Fixed-term Parliaments Act 2011, general elections must normally be held on the first Thursday in May every five years1 (although see paragraphs 2.2 and 2.3 below). Parliament is dissolved before such an election. Dissolution occurs automatically, 17 working days before the next election (see paragraph 2.22 for more on dissolution). Parliament meets on the date determined by the issue by Her Majesty in Council of a proclamation summoning a new Parliament. That date may be postponed by a subsequent proclamation under the Prorogation Act 1867.2

2.2   Once Parliament is dissolved, the Fixed term Parliaments Act 2011 gives authority for the issue of writs for the election of a new House of Commons (a writ is a formal written order). Writs are issued under the Representation of the People Act 1983 by the Clerk of the Crown in Chancery, who is also Permanent Secretary to the Ministry of Justice, to Returning Officers in Great Britain, and by the Clerk of the Crown for Northern Ireland to Returning Officers in Northern Ireland, and require them to cause elections to be held and to return the writ with the election result for their constituency. Writs of summons are also issued to all Members of the House of Lords to summon them to a new Parliament.

2.3   The election process and a more detailed election timetable (derived from the Representation of the People Act 1983) is set out at the annex to this Manual. Candidates must submit nomination papers not later than the sixth working day after the date of the dissolution of Parliament.3

Meeting of the new Parliament

2.4   The date of the first meeting of a new Parliament is determined by a proclamation issued by the Sovereign, on the advice of the Prime Minister. Recent practice had been for Parliament to meet on the Wednesday following the election. In 2007, the Select Committee on the Modernisation of the House of Commons recommended a reversion to the previous practice of having an interval of 12 days between polling day and the first meeting of Parliament.4This was adopted in 2010.

2.5   The first business of the House of Commons when it meets is to elect or re-elect a Speaker and for Members to take the oath.5 The first business of the House of Lords is also for its Members to take the oath.6Normally the Queen's Speech outlining the Government's legislative programme will take place in the second week of Parliament's sitting and is followed by four or five days of debate.7This is when the business of the new Parliament properly begins.

2.6   The election of the Lord Speaker is not dependent on a general election: it takes place on a day no later than 15 July in the fifth calendar year after the previous election of the Lord Speaker. The last took place on 13 July 2011. Where a dissolution of Parliament has been announced the election either takes place on the date set for the election of a new Lord Speaker or on a day no later than one month after the State Opening, whichever is later.8

The principles of government formation

2.7   The ability of a government to command the confidence of the elected House of Commons is central to its authority to govern. It is tested by votes on motions of confidence, or no confidence.9See paragraph 2.19 on fixed-term Parliaments and votes of no confidence. Commanding the confidence of the House of Commons is not the same as having a majority or winning every vote.

2.8   Prime Ministers hold office unless and until they resign. If the Prime Minister resigns on behalf of the Government, the Sovereign will invite the person who appears most likely to be able to command the confidence of the House to serve as Prime Minister and to form a government.10

2.9   Historically, the Sovereign has made use of reserve powers to dismiss a Prime Minister or to make a personal choice of successor, although this was last used in 1834 and was regarded as having undermined the Sovereign.11In modern times the convention has been that the Sovereign should not be drawn into party politics, and if there is doubt it is the responsibility of those involved in the political process, and in particular the parties represented in Parliament, to seek to determine and communicate clearly to the Sovereign who is best placed to be able to command the confidence of the House of Commons. As the Crown's principal adviser this responsibility falls especially on the incumbent Prime Minister, who at the time of his or her resignation may also be asked by the Sovereign for a recommendation on who can best command the confidence of the House of Commons in his or her place.

2.10 The application of these principles depends on the specific circumstances and it remains a matter for the Prime Minister, as the Sovereign's principal adviser, to judge the appropriate time at which to resign, either from their individual position as Prime Minister or on behalf of the government.12 Recent examples suggest that previous Prime Ministers have not offered their resignations until there was a situation in which clear advice could be given to the Sovereign on who should be asked to form a government.13 It remains to be seen whether or not these examples will be regarded in future as having established a constitutional convention. Parliaments with an overall majority in the House of Commons

2.11 After an election, if an incumbent government retains an overall majority – that is, where the number of seats won by the largest party in an election exceeds the combined number of seats for all the other parties in the new Parliament – it will normally continue in office and resume normal business. There is no need for the Sovereign to ask the Prime Minister to continue. If the election results in an overall majority for a different party, the incumbent Prime Minister and government will immediately resign and the Sovereign will invite the leader of the party that has won the election to form a government. Details on the appointment of the Prime Minister and ministers can be found in Chapter Three. Parliaments with no overall majority in the House of Commons

2.12 Where an election does not result in an overall majority for a single party, the incumbent government remains in office unless and until the Prime Minister tenders his or her resignation and the Government's resignation to the Sovereign. An incumbent government is entitled to wait until the new Parliament has met to see if it can command the confidence of the House of Commons, but is expected to resign if it becomes clear that it is unlikely to be able to command that confidence and there is a clear alternative.

2.13 Where a range of different administrations could potentially be formed, political parties may wish to hold discussions to establish who is best able to command the confidence of the House of Commons and should form the next government. The Sovereign would not expect to become involved in any negotiations, although there are responsibilities on those involved in the process to keep the Palace informed. This could be done by political parties or the Cabinet Secretary. The Principal Private Secretary to the Prime Minister may also have a role, for example, in communicating with the Palace.

2.14 If the leaders of the political parties involved in any negotiations seek the support of the Civil Service, this support may only be organised by the Cabinet Secretary with the authorisation of the Prime Minister. If the Prime Minister authorises any support it would be focused and provided on an equal basis to all the parties involved, including the party that was currently in government. The Civil Service would continue to advise the incumbent government in the usual way.

2.15 Following the election in May 2010, the Prime Minister authorised the Civil Service to provide such support to negotiations between political parties.14

2.16 As long as there is significant doubt following an election over the Government's ability to command the confidence of the House of Commons, certain restrictions on government activity apply; see paragraphs 2.27–2.34.

2.17 The nature of the government formed will be dependent on discussions between political parties and any resulting agreement. Where there is no overall majority, there are essentially three broad types of government that could be formed:

- Single-party, minority government, where the party may (although not necessarily) be supported by a series of ad hoc agreements based on common interests;

- formal inter-party agreement, for example the Liberal–Labour pact from 1977 to 1978; or

- formal coalition government, which generally consists of ministers from more than one political party, and typically commands a majority in the House of Commons.15

Change of Prime Minister or government during a Parliament

2.18 Where a Prime Minister chooses to resign from his or her individual position at a time when his or her administration has an overall majority in the House of Commons, it is for the party or parties in government to identify who can be chosen as the successor.16

2.19 Under the Fixed-term Parliaments Act 2011, if a government is defeated on a motion that 'this House has no confidence in Her Majesty's Government', there is then a 14-day period during which an alternative government can be formed from the House of Commons as presently constituted, or the incumbent government can seek to regain the confidence of the House.17 If no government can secure the confidence of the House of Commons during that period, through the approval of a motion that 'this House has confidence in Her Majesty's Government', a general election will take place. Other decisions of the House of Commons which have previously been regarded as expressing 'no confidence' in the government no longer enable or require the Prime Minister to hold a general election. The Prime Minister is expected to resign where it is clear that he or she does not have the confidence of the House of Commons and that an alternative government does have the confidence.

2.20 Where a range of different administrations could be formed, discussions may take place between political parties on who should form the next government. In these circumstances the processes and considerations described in paragraphs 2.12–2.17 would apply.

Pre-election contact with opposition parties

2.21 At an appropriate time towards the end of any Parliament, as the next general election approaches, the Prime Minister writes to the leaders of the main opposition parties to authorise pre-election contacts with the Civil Service.18

The meetings take place on a confidential basis, without ministers being present or receiving a report of discussions. The Cabinet Secretary has overall responsibility for co-ordinating this process once a request has been made and authorised by the Prime Minister. These discussions are designed to allow the Opposition's shadow ministers to ask questions about departmental organisation and to inform civil servants of any organisational changes likely to take place in the event of a change of government. Senior civil servants may ask questions about the implications of opposition parties' policy statements, although they would not normally comment on or give advice about policies.

Dissolution of Parliament

2.22 Parliaments dissolve automatically 17 working days before the date of the next election.19 This date will ordinarily be the first Thursday in May five years after the day on which the Parliament was elected, unless an early election is held in accordance with the provisions of the Fixed-term Parliaments Act 2011 or the Prime Minister has exercised his or her power to defer the election by up to two months because of an emergency. No further formality is required for dissolution in accordance with the Act, but a proclamation is required to summon a new Parliament for a specified date.

2.23 Early elections may take place in two circumstances. The first is where two thirds of the membership of the House of Commons agree that it is right that there should be a general election immediately and pass a motion 'that there shall be an early Parliamentary general election'. The other circumstance is where a government has lost a motion that 'this House has no confidence in Her Majesty's Government' and no government has, within a 14-day period, secured a motion that 'this House has confidence in Her Majesty's Government'. In either of these cases, the date of the election is set by the Sovereign by Proclamation on the advice of the Prime Minister and dissolution occurs 17 working days before the date appointed for the election. Proclamations are issued by Her Majesty in Council.

2.24 Parliament may be prorogued before being dissolved or may just adjourn. It has not been modern practice for Parliament to be dissolved while sitting. Prorogation brings a Parliamentary session to an end. It is the Sovereign who prorogues Parliament on the advice of his or her ministers. The normal procedure is for commissioners appointed by the Sovereign to prorogue Parliament in accordance with an Order in Council. The commissioners also declare Royal Assent to the bills that have passed both Houses, so that they become Acts, and then they announce the prorogation to both Houses in the House of Lords.20

2.25 It is not necessary for Parliament to have been prorogued in order for it to be dissolved. In 1992, 1997, 2005 and 2010 Parliament was dissolved following prorogation, but in 2001 and for all the elections in the 1970s and 1980s after the 1970 election, Parliament was dissolved while adjourned without a prorogation. Finalisation of Parliamentary business

2.26 Where an early general election takes place, the date appointed for the poll may enable Parliament to sit for a few days before dissolution, known as the 'wash-up' period. Dissolution occurs automatically 17 working days before the date appointed for the election. Some business may have to be completed before the dissolution. In particular, any money voted to the Government but not appropriated has to be appropriated by the date of the dissolution21and, depending on the time of year, it may be necessary to do other business to keep government working while Parliament is unavailable because of the dissolution.

Restrictions on government activity

2.27 While the government retains its responsibility to govern and ministers remain in charge of their departments, governments are expected by convention to observe discretion in initiating any new action of a continuing or long-term character in the period immediately preceding an election, immediately afterwards if the result is unclear, and following the loss of a vote of confidence. In all three circumstances essential business must be allowed to continue.22

Government activity between the start of an election period and polling day

2.28 In the period immediately preceding an election, the Cabinet Office publishes guidance on activities in the run up to polling day.23 The Prime Minister writes to ministers in similar terms.

2.29 During this period, the government retains its responsibility to govern, ministers remain in charge of their departments and essential business is carried on.24Ministers continue in office and it is customary for them to observe discretion in initiating any action of a continuing or long-term character. This means the deferral of activity such as: taking or announcing major policy decisions; entering into large/contentious procurement contracts or significant long-term commitments; and making some senior public appointments and approving Senior Civil Service appointments, provided that such postponement would not be detrimental to the national interest or wasteful of public money. If decisions cannot wait they may be handled by temporary arrangements or following relevant consultation with the Opposition.

Activity post election

2.30 Immediately following an election, if there is no overall majority, for as long as there is significant doubt over the Government's ability to command the confidence of the House of Commons, many of the restrictions set out at paragraphs 2.27–2.29 would continue to apply. The point at which the restrictions on financial and other commitments should come to an end depends on circumstances, but may often be either when a new Prime Minister is appointed by the Sovereign or where a government's ability to command the confidence of the Commons has been tested in the House of Commons.

Activity following loss of confidence

2.31 If a government loses a vote that 'this House has no confidence in His or Her Majesty's Government', it will remain in office during the government formation period of up to 14 days, until a government has secured the confidence of the House of Commons, or no government has secured such confidence and Parliament is dissolved 17 working days before the date set for the early general election. During that period the restrictions in paragraphs 2.27–2.29 would apply.

Directions during a period of restrictions on government activity

2.32 The rules under which an accounting officer may seek a direction from a minister (where the officer has an objection to a proposed course of action on grounds of propriety, regularity or value for money relating to proposed expenditure) continue to apply during the three periods described above. The principles set out in paragraphs 2.27–2.29, as appropriate, will be relevant to the application of those rules.

2.33 In normal circumstances (as set out in Chapter Ten: Government finance and expenditure), a ministerial direction to an accounting officer is sent to the Comptroller and Auditor General (C&AG) who will normally forward it to the Committee of Public Accounts. It should also be copied to the Treasury Officer of Accounts. During any period when Parliament is prorogued or dissolved, if the occasion for any such directions arose, and taking account of issues of commercial or other sensitivity, the direction, together with the reasoning provided by the accounting officer, should be made public immediately by the department and laid before both Houses at the first opportunity after Parliament meets. The direction should also be sent to the C&AG and copied to the Treasury Officer of Accounts at the time of publication.

Other elections

2.34 Some more limited restrictions on government activity also apply during other elections: to the European Parliament, the Devolved Administrations and local government. The guidance issued by the Cabinet Office for the May 2011 elections provides an example.25

Notes

1   Fixed-term Parliaments Act 2011, s.1(3).

2   Jack M (ed.) (2011) Erskine May's Treatise on the Law, Privileges, Proceedings and Usage of Parliament, 24th edition. London: LexisNexis Butterworths, p. 146.

3   Representation of the People Act 1983, Schedule 1, paragraph 1.

4   Select Committee on Modernisation of the House of Commons (2007) Revitalising the Chamber: the role of the back bench Member (HC337). London: The Stationery Office.

5   Jack (ed.) Erskine May, pp. 150–154.

6   Ibid., pp. 501–502.

7   Ibid., pp. 157–162.

8   House of Lords, Standing Order 19.

9   The minimum majority for a confidence vote is 50% + 1 of those present and voting.

10   Rarely, a Prime Minister may resign and then be asked to form a new administration. For example, Ramsay MacDonald resigned as Prime Minister of a Labour government and was reappointed as Prime Minister of a National Government in 1931. Winston Churchill was also asked to form a new Conservative administration following the break-up of the wartime coalition government in 1945.

11   William IV dismissed Lord Melbourne's government that had majority support in the House of Commons.

12   It has been suggested in evidence to select committees that the incumbent Prime Minister's responsibility involves a duty to remain in office until it is clear who should be appointed in their place (Political and Constitutional Reform Committee (2011) Lessons from the process of Government formation after the 2010 General Election (HC528).

London: The Stationery Office, paragraphs 16–22). Whether the responsibilities of the Prime Minister in these circumstances amount to a duty and how far they extend has been questioned, and the House of Lords Constitution Committee concluded that an incumbent Prime Minister has no duty to remain in office following an inconclusive general election until it is clear what form any alternative government might take. (House of Lords Constitution Committee (2011) 12th Report: The Cabinet Manual (HL107). London: The Stationery Office, paragraph 61).

13   Margaret Thatcher's resignation statement on 22 November 1990 said that she had informed Her Majesty the Queen that she did not intend to contest the second ballot of the election for leadership of the Conservative Party and gave notice of her intention to resign as Prime Minister as soon as a new leader had been elected. She formally tendered her resignation on 28 November 1990. On 10 May 2007 Tony Blair announced his intention to resign once a new leader of the Labour Party had been elected. He formally tendered his resignation on 27 June 2007. Following the 2010 general election, which took place on 6 May, Gordon Brown resigned on 11 May, by when it was clear that David Cameron should be asked to form a government.

14   The Civil Service was authorised to provide: advice on the constitutional processes of government formation; factual information in relation to speciic policy proposals; and facilitation of discussions and negotiations (including the provision of facilities such as meeting rooms). Further information on the nature of

that support can be found at: www.cabinetofice.gov.uk/resource-library/civil-service-support-coalition-negotiations.

15   The Conservative Party and the Liberal Democrat Party coalition, formed in May 2010, is the most recent example of a UK coalition government. Further detail of how the coalition operates in practice and the procedures that apply are set out in the Government's Coalition Agreement for Stability and Reform (2010), which includes detail on the composition of the Government and the application of collective responsibility. This, and The Coalition: our programme for government (2010), can be found at: www.cabinetofice.gov.uk/news/coalition-documents.

16   See note 13.

17   Fixed-term Parliaments Act 2011, s.2(3).

18   Cabinet Office (2000) Directory of Civil Service Guidance, Volume 2. London: Cabinet Office, pp. 18 and 19. For example, pre-election contacts were authorised from 1 January 2009 for the election held in May 2010. For the election held in June 2005 (which could have been held as late as July 2006), contacts had been authorised from 1 January 2005.

19   Fixed-term Parliaments Act 2011, s.3(1).

20   Jack (ed.) Erskine May, paragraph 145.

21   Ibid., pp. 742–743.

22   Cabinet Office (May 2011) Elections Guidance, paragraph 3.

23   The most recent guidance to government departments issued in relation to a general election is Cabinet Office (2010) Elections Guidance.

24   In some previous elections this has been done through an Election Business Committee.

25   Cabinet Office (2011) Elections Guidance.

Chapter Three

The Prime Minister is head of the Government by virtue of his or her ability to command the confidence of the House of Commons. He or she is appointed by the Sovereign and in turn recommends to the Sovereign the appointment of ministers to the Government.

This chapter covers:

- The Prime Minister
- Ministers
- Powers of ministers
- Ministerial conduct
- The structure of government.

The Executive – the Prime Minister, ministers and the structure of government

The Prime Minister

3.1 The Prime Minister is the head of the Government and holds that position by virtue of his or her ability to command the confidence of the House of Commons, which in turn commands the confidence of the electorate, as expressed through a general election. The Prime Minister's unique position of authority also comes from support in the House of Commons. By modern convention, the Prime Minister always sits in the House of Commons.1 The Prime Minister will normally be the accepted leader of a political party that commands the majority of the House of Commons. For cases where no political party has an overall majority, see Chapter Two, paragraphs 2.12–2.17.

3.2 The Prime Minister accepts office at a private audience with the Sovereign, at which time the appointment takes effect. The Prime Minister is, by tradition, the First Lord of the Treasury (for more information on the Treasury Commissioners and the First Lord of the Treasury see paragraph 3.29). In his or her capacity as First Lord of the Treasury, the Prime Minister takes oaths of office under the Promissory Oaths Act 1868.2

3.3 The Prime Minister has few statutory functions but will usually take the lead on significant matters of state. The Prime Minister has certain prerogatives, for example recommending the appointment of ministers and determining the membership of Cabinet and Cabinet committees. However, in some circumstances the Prime Minister may agree to consult others before exercising those prerogatives.3 The Ministerial Code states: 'the Prime Minister is responsible for the overall organisation of the Executive and the allocation of functions between Ministers in charge of departments.'4

3.4 It is for the Prime Minister to advise the Sovereign on the exercise of the Royal Prerogative powers in relation to government, such as the appointment, dismissal and acceptance of resignation of other ministers and certain statutory powers, such as the calling of elections where there is an early election or a deferred election under the Fixed-term Parliaments Act 2011 (see the section on ministers' powers below).

3.5   At regular meetings with the Sovereign, the Prime Minister informs him or her of the general business of the government. The Prime Minister's other responsibilities include recommending a number of appointments to the Sovereign. These include high-ranking members of the Church of England, senior judges and certain civil appointments. He or she also recommends appointments to several public boards and institutions, as well as to various Royal and statutory commissions. 21

3.6   The Prime Minister has held the office of Minister for the Civil Service since that office was created in 1968, in which capacity he or she has overall responsibility for the management of most of the Civil Service (see Chapter Seven: Ministers and the Civil Service).5 The Prime Minister is the minister responsible for National Security and matters affecting the Secret Intelligence Service,

Security Service and GCHQ collectively, in addition to which the Home and Foreign Secretaries of State and the Secretary of State for Northern Ireland have powers granted in legislation to authorise specific operations.6 The Prime Minister is also sworn as a member of the Privy Council.

Ministers

3.7   In general, the ministers in the government can be divided into the following categories: senior ministers; junior ministers; the Law Officers; and whips. The Prime Minister may agree that a minister in any of the categories can be known by a 'courtesy title' reflecting the job the minister has been asked to do, for example 'Minister for Europe'. A courtesy title has no legal or constitutional significance.

3.8   There is a convention that an individual will be a minister only if they are a Member of the House of Commons or the House of Lords, with most being Members of the House of Commons. However, there are examples of individuals being appointed as a minister in anticipation of their becoming a Member of one of the Houses and of continuing to hold office for a short period after ceasing to be Members of the House of Commons.7

Senior ministers

3.9   The most senior ministers in the Government are the members of Cabinet. The Prime Minister determines who forms Cabinet, but this will always include the Chancellor of the Exchequer, the Lord Chancellor and the secretaries of state. There are no formal limits on the size of Cabinet, but there are limits on the number of ministerial salaries that can be paid, and particularly who can be paid first-tier (Cabinet-level) salaries (see paragraph 3.23).

3.10 Other ministers who are often invited by the Prime Minister to be a member of, or attend, Cabinet include the Lord President of the Council, the Lord Privy Seal, the Chancellor of the Duchy of Lancaster, the Paymaster General, the Chief Secretary to the Treasury and the Parliamentary Secretary to the Treasury (the Commons Chief Whip). A minister of state may also sometimes be invited to be a member of, or attend, Cabinet.

The Deputy Prime Minister

3.11 The title of Deputy Prime Minister is sometimes given to a senior minister in the Government, for example the deputy leader of the party in government or the leader of the smaller party in a coalition. The role of the Deputy Prime Minister is sometimes combined with other roles, but responsibilities will vary according to the circumstances. For example, in 2010 the role of the Deputy Prime Minister was combined with that of Lord President of the Council, with ministerial responsibility for political and constitutional reform. The fact that a person has the title of Deputy Prime Minister does not constrain the Sovereign's power to appoint a successor to a Prime Minister.

The First Secretary of State

3.12   A minister may be appointed First Secretary of State to indicate seniority. The appointment may be held with another office. The responsibilities of the First Secretary of State will vary according to the circumstances. For more about the secretaries of state, see paragraphs 3.26–3.28.

Junior ministers

3.13 Junior ministers are generally ministers of state, Parliamentary under secretaries of state and Parliamentary secretaries. Typically they are ministers within a government department and their function is to support and assist the senior minister in charge of the department. See paragraphs 3.40–3.44 on the Carltona principle, under which junior ministers in a department may exercise statutory functions of the minister in charge of the department.

Law Officers

3.14 The UK Law Officers are:

- the Attorney General
- the Solicitor General
- the Advocate General for Scotland
- the Advocate General for Northern Ireland.

3.15 The role of the Law Officers is covered in more detail in Chapter Six.

Whips

3.16 Government whips are appointed for both the House of Commons and the House of Lords. The government chief whips in the House of Commons and the House of Lords arrange the scheduling of government business, often in consultation with their opposition counterparts. Collectively, the government and opposition whips are often referred to as 'the usual channels' when the question of finding time for a particular item of business is being discussed.8

3.17 The chief whips and their assistants manage their Parliamentary parties. Their duties include keeping members informed of forthcoming Parliamentary business, maintaining the party's voting strength by ensuring that members attend important votes, and passing on to the party leadership the opinions of backbench members. Whips in the House of Commons do not generally speak during Parliamentary debates. However, Lords whips may speak in Parliament on behalf of departments.

Appointment of ministers

3.18 Senior ministers are required to take oaths of office under the Promissory Oaths Act 18689 and all Cabinet members are made Privy Counsellors.

3.19 Secretaries of state and some other ministers (for example, the Lord Privy Seal) also receive seals of office. Their appointments take effect by the delivery of those seals by the Sovereign. Others have their appointments made or confirmed by Letters Patent (for example, the Attorney General) or Royal Warrant (for example, the Paymaster General). Appointments of other ministers generally take effect from when the Sovereign accepts the Prime Minister's recommendation of the appointment. For more details on Privy Council appointments, see Chapter One.

Resignation of ministers

3.20 Ministers may resign when they are not able to continue to accept collective responsibility, or because of issues relating to their conduct in office, or due to a personal or private matter. Where a minister resigns their post by writing to the Prime Minister, it is often the case that the exchange of letters is published.

Parliamentary private secretaries

3.21 Cabinet ministers and ministers of state may appoint Parliamentary private secretaries. All appointments require the prior written approval of the Prime Minister. The Chief Whip should also be consulted and no commitments to make such appointments should be entered into until such approval is received.10

3.22 Parliamentary private secretaries are not members of the Government, although by convention they are bound by collective agreement.11 Their role is to support ministers in conducting Parliamentary business.

Limits on ministerial numbers and salaries

3.23 The Ministerial and other Salaries Act 1975 limits the number of paid ministers (whether sitting in the House of Commons or the House of Lords) to 109.12 Under the House of Commons Disqualification Act 1975, there is a maximum of 95 ministers, paid or unpaid, who may sit in the House of Commons.13 Parliamentary private secretaries do not count towards the limit on House of Commons ministers or the limits on salaries.

Powers of ministers

3.24 Ministers' powers derive from: Parliament, which grants powers through legislation; ministers' common law powers to act; and prerogative powers of the Crown that are exercised by, or on the advice of, ministers. Each form of power is subject to 23 The Cabinet Manual limits and constraints, and its use may be challenged in the courts. Ministers can also only spend public money for the purposes authorised by Parliament (see Chapter Ten: government finance and expenditure). Powers may be exercised by civil servants on behalf of ministers (see paragraphs 3.40–3.44).

Powers granted by Parliament

3.25 Many Acts of Parliament grant powers to ministers or place statutory duties on ministers.14 Normal practice is that the powers and duties involved in exercising continuing functions of ministers (particularly those involving financial liabilities extending beyond a given year) should be identified in legislation.15 Statute also provides ministers with emergency powers, in particular that emergency regulations could be made by Order in Council or by ministers as a last resort where existing legislation is insufficient to respond in the most effective way.16

3.26 Most statutory powers and duties are conferred on the Secretary of State; these may be exercised or complied with by any one of the secretaries of state.17 This reflects the doctrine that there is only one office of Secretary of State, even though it is the well-established practice to appoint more than one person to carry out the functions of the office.

3.27 It is also the well-established practice for each secretary of state to be allocated responsibility by the Prime Minister for a particular department (for example health, foreign affairs, defence, transport, education etc.) and, accordingly, for each Secretary of State, in practice, to exercise only those functions that are within that department. It is for the Prime Minister to determine the various departments (see paragraphs 3.55–3.59 on machinery of government changes).

3.28 Most secretaries of state are incorporated as 'corporations sole'. This gives the minister a separate legal personality. This is administratively convenient, for example as regards the ownership of property, because it facilitates continuity when the officeholder changes.

3.29 Statutory powers conferred on the Treasury are exercisable by the Commissioners of the Treasury,18 and may not be exercised by other ministers. The First Lord of the Treasury, along with the Chancellor of the Exchequer and the Junior Lords of the Treasury, make up the Commissioners of Her Majesty's Treasury. However, the Treasury Commissioners do not meet in that capacity. In practice, the Treasury is headed by the Chancellor of the Exchequer supported by the Chief Secretary to the Treasury and other junior Treasury ministers.

3.30 Other powers are conferred on a specific minister and may only be exercised by that minister. For example, a number of powers in relation to the judiciary are specifically conferred on the Lord Chancellor. While statutory powers may be conferred on individual ministers, in practice the exercise of those powers is normally subject to collective agreement. Paragraph 4.16 in Chapter Four sets out the circumstances in which collective agreement applies, and the exceptions to collective agreement are at paragraphs 4.23–4.25 of that chapter.

Inherent or 'common law' powers

3.31 Ministers' functions are not limited to those authorised by statute. A minister may, as an agent of the Crown, exercise any powers which the Crown may exercise, except insofar as ministers are precluded from doing so by statute and subject to the fact that a minister will only be able to pay for what he or she does if Parliament votes him or her the money. This is a summary of what is known as the Ram doctrine.19

3.32 The powers that a minister may exercise include any of the legal powers of an individual, for example to enter into contracts, convey property or make extra statutory payments. As more of ministers' powers have been codified in legislation, the extent of inherent powers has been correspondingly reduced.

Prerogative powers

3.33 Prerogative powers are generally exercised by ministers or by the Sovereign on the advice of ministers, particularly the Prime Minister. However, the Sovereign continues to exercise personally some prerogative powers of the Crown (the award of certain honours, such as the Order of Merit) and reserves the right to exercise others in unusual circumstances (see paragraph 1.5).

3.34 Prerogative powers may be divided into the following broad categories:

- Constitutional or personal prerogatives: these are the powers that the Sovereign continues to exercise either personally or on the advice of the Government. They include the powers to: appoint and dismiss the Prime Minister and other ministers; grant assent to legislation; and prorogue Parliament.

- Prerogative executive powers: these are the powers that are exercised on the Sovereign's behalf by ministers. Most prerogative powers fall into this category. They include powers in relation to foreign affairs, to deploy the Armed Forces and to grant mercy. The limited prerogative powers that are relevant to devolved functions are exercised by ministers in the Devolved Administrations.

3.35 The scope of the prerogative is affected both by the common law (as developed by the courts) and by statutes (as enacted by Parliament) and accordingly has changed over time.20

3.36 The role of the courts in determining the existence and extent of the prerogative from time to time can be a significant control on the prerogative. In particular, the control is strengthened by the common law doctrine that courts cannot create new prerogatives.21Equally; however, the courts can recognise prerogatives that were previously of doubtful provenance, or adapt old prerogatives to modern circumstances. For example, the Secretary of State's prerogative power to act to maintain law and order where no emergency exists was not widely recognised until identified by the Court of Appeal in 1989.22

3.37 Over time, legislation has also clarified and limited the extent of the prerogative, including in some cases abolishing it.23

Some Acts passed in recent years, although not primarily aimed at reforming the prerogative, have nevertheless brought about significant reforms. For example, historically there has been a prerogative power in times of emergency to enter upon, take and destroy private property.

The Civil Contingencies Act 2004 in practice covers the majority of situations where it might previously have been appropriate to use the prerogative.

3.38 Departmental civil servants provide advice to ministers on the extent of their powers. In the most complex cases, reference can be made to the Law Officers (see Chapter Six).

Role of the courts in scrutinizing the exercise of ministers' powers

3.39 The courts scrutinise the manner in which powers are exercised. The main route is through the mechanism of judicial review, which enables the actions of a minister to be challenged on the basis that he or she did not have the power to act in such a way (including on human rights grounds); that the action was unreasonable; or that the power was exercised in a procedurally unfair way. For information on judicial review, see paragraphs 6.10–6.13 in Chapter Six.

Exercise of ministers' powers

3.40 Generally speaking, junior ministers in a ministerial department and civil servants working for a departmental minister may exercise powers of the minister in charge of the department, under what is known as the Carltona principle.

3.41 The principle derives from the case Carltona Ltd v Commissioners of Works.24 The Court of Appeal recognised that ministers' functions are normally exercised under the authority of the minister by responsible officials of the department and that public business could not be carried on if that were not so. The Court considered that, in such cases, decisions of officials are to be regarded, constitutionally, as decisions of the minister rather than as decisions of someone to whom the minister has delegated the function.

3.42 Although decisions are treated as decisions of the minister, the Carltona principle can be regarded as providing an exception, in practice, to the rule that a statutory function conferred on a particular person cannot in general be delegated to another person without express or implied statutory authority.

3.43 The Carltona principle does not apply where the courts infer an intention on the part of Parliament that the named minister should act personally – for example with some quasi-judicial functions. In any case, ministers will require all major decisions to be referred to them.

3.44 Under Part 2 of the Deregulation and Contracting Out Act 1994, a minister may authorise any person (whether or not a civil servant) to exercise the minister's functions. The Act applies only to functions that are conferred on the minister by or under an enactment and can be exercised by a civil servant in the minister's department (for example under the Carltona principle). Some categories of functions are excluded – for example functions that necessarily affect the liberty of an individual and powers to make subordinate legislation. A minister may authorise a person to exercise a ministerial function only if the function is specified in an order made under the Act. The exercise of a function by a person authorised under the Act is treated for most purposes as the exercise of the function by the minister.

3.45 Ministers remain accountable to Parliament for the decisions made under their powers.25

Ministerial conduct

3.46 The Ministerial Code, issued by the Prime Minister of the day, sets out the principles underpinning the standards of conduct expected of ministers. Ministers of the Crown are expected to behave in a way that upholds the highest standards of propriety, including ensuring that no conflict arises or appears to arise, between their public duties and their private interests.26

Ministers are under an overarching duty to comply with the law, including international law and treaty obligations, uphold the administration of justice and protect the integrity of public life. They are expected to observe the Seven Principles of Public Life: selflessness, integrity, objectivity, accountability, openness, honesty and leadership.27

3.47 On leaving office, former ministers must seek advice from the independent Advisory Committee on Business Appointments about any appointments or employment they wish to take up within two years of leaving office. The advice of the Committee is made public when the appointment is taken up or announced. The Ministerial Code makes it clear that former ministers must abide by the advice of the Committee. Former ministers are currently prohibited from lobbying government for two years.28

The structure of government

Allocation of functions to ministers

3.48 The Prime Minister is responsible for the overall organisation of the Government and the allocation of functions between ministers. It is a fundamental part of the Prime Minister's role to ensure that Cabinet and the Government are structured in the most effective way.

Government departments

3.49 As powers generally rest with the Secretary of State and departments do not have their own legal personality, the structure of government departments tends to change to reflect the allocation of functions to ministers.

3.50 Most government departments are headed by a Secretary of State and will carry out the functions which the Prime Minister has allocated to that Secretary of State or which are conferred specifically on that Secretary of State by legislation. Other ministerial departments are headed by another senior minister (for example the Chancellor of the Exchequer in the case of the Treasury).

3.51 Government departments generally have one or more junior ministers who are usually allocated specific areas of responsibility within which they carry out functions in the name of the department's senior minister. The roles of junior ministers 26 Chapter Three may be set by the Prime Minister when they are appointed (for example as the 'Minister for Trade and Investment'), or functions may be allocated by a Secretary of State to the junior ministers within his or her department.

Arm's-length bodies

3.52 Arm's-length bodies are public bodies established to carry out specific central government functions at arm's length from ministers. There are three main types of arm's-length body:29

• Non-ministerial departments (NMDs) are central government departments staffed by civil servants. NMDs have a board and ministers do not have direct control over them. Instead they have a sponsoring minister, who typically appoints the board.

• Executive agencies are well-defined units with a focus on delivering specific outcomes. They are part of a department and are staffed by civil servants.

• Non-departmental public bodies are bodies that have a role in the processes of national government, but are not government departments or part of one, and operate to a greater or lesser extent at arm's length from ministers. They are usually set up as separate legal entities, such as statutory bodies, and employ their own staff, who are not civil servants.

3.53 The role and responsibilities of ministers in relation to individual arm's-length bodies are usually set out in framework documents.30

3.54 Existing arm's-length bodies are regularly reviewed and proposals for new arm's-length bodies must be approved by the Cabinet Office.

Machinery of government changes

3.55 The Prime Minister has responsibility for machinery of government changes.31 The Prime Minister's written approval must be sought where it is proposed by ministers to transfer functions:

• between ministers in charge of departments, unless the changes are minor and can be made administratively and do not justify public announcement;

• within the field of ministerial responsibility of one minister, when the change is likely to be politically sensitive or to raise wider issues of policy or organisation; or

• between junior ministers within a department, when a change in ministerial titles is involved.32

3.56 The Prime Minister's approval should also be sought for proposals to allocate new functions to a particular minister where the function does not fall wholly within the field of responsibilities of one minister, or where there is a disagreement about who should be responsible. In addition, a ministerial head of department's proposal for the assignment of duties to junior ministers, together with any proposed courtesy titles descriptive of their duties should be agreed in writing with the Prime Minister. The establishment of an NMD is considered a machinery of government change.

3.57 A transfer of functions order (an Order in Council under the Ministers of the Crown Act 1975) is likely to be needed for major changes involving ministerial departments. In some cases, usually where there is a transfer of statutory functions to or from a specific departmental minister such as the Lord Chancellor, it will not be possible to implement the change until the order is made. Where the change is a reallocation between secretaries of state of functions expressed to be exercisable by 'the Secretary of State', it will usually be possible to implement the change in advance of the order being made. Primary legislation may be needed for machinery of government changes extending beyond a ministerial department. The Office of the Parliamentary Counsel is responsible for drafting transfer of functions orders.

3.58 The Cabinet Secretary is responsible for advising the Prime Minister on machinery of government issues. Departments involved in machinery of government changes, or considering proposing such changes to the Prime Minister, should consult the Cabinet Secretariat for advice.

3.59 While the allocation of functions to ministers is a matter for the Prime Minister, the Government informs Parliament of significant machinery of government changes. The Cabinet Office publishes an explanatory document about major changes on the Cabinet Office website and arranges for it to be placed in the libraries of both Houses. This helps explain to Parliament and the public the Prime

Minister's reasoning for making the changes. Ministers usually make themselves available to any relevant select committee that wishes to examine the implementation of such changes.

Notes

1   Prime Ministers in previous centuries have sat in the House of Lords, for example the Marquess of Salisbury who was a member of the House of Lords and was Prime Minister for periods in the late 19th century and early 20th century.

2   Promissory Oaths Act 1868, s.5.

3   For example, under the Coalition Agreement for Stability and Reform (2010) the Prime Minister agreed that a number of prerogative powers, including the appointment of ministers and ministerial functions allocation, would only be exercised after consultation with the Deputy Prime Minister.

4   Cabinet Ofice (2010) Ministerial Code, paragraph 4.1.

5   Constitutional Reform and Governance Act 2010, s.3.

6   Security Service Act 1989; Regulation of Investigatory Powers Act 2000; Intelligence Services Act 1994; further information is available at: www.sis.gov.uk/about-us/sis-in-government.html.

7   Patrick Gordon Walker was appointed as Foreign Secretary in October 1964 after losing his Parliamentary seat in the general election. He resigned in January 1965 after being defeated in the Leyton by-election. Before devolution, the Solicitor General for Scotland was often not a Member of the House of Commons or the House of Lords.

8   For more information on whips, see: House of Commons Library (2008) The Whip's Office, Standard Note SN/PC/02829.

9   Promissory Oaths Act 1868, s.5.

10   Cabinet Office, Ministerial Code, paragraph 3.6.

11   Ibid., paragraph 3.9.

12   Ministerial and Other Salaries Act 1975, Schedule 1.

13   House of Commons Disqualification Act 1975, Schedule 2.

14   Examples of provisions imposing duties on a minister are sections 5 and 6 of the Constitutional Reform and Governance Act 2010, which require the Minister for the Civil Service to publish codes of conduct for the Civil Service and Diplomatic Service, and section 7 of that Act, which imposes requirements as to their content. An example of a provision conferring a power on a minister is section 19 of the Companies Act 2006, which gives the Secretary of State power to prescribe model articles of association for companies.

15   HM Treasury (2011) Managing Public Money, Annex 2.1; Public Accounts Committee Concordat 1932.

16   Civil Contingencies Act 2004, ss.19–31.

17   'Secretary of State' is deined in Schedule 1 to the Interpretation Act 1978 as meaning 'one of Her Majesty's Principal Secretaries of State' (unless a contrary intention appears).

18   'The Treasury' is deined in Schedule 1 to the Interpretation Act 1978 as meaning 'the Commissioners of Her Majesty's Treasury'.

19   The Ram doctrine is set out in a memorandum dated 2 November 1945 from Granville Ram, Ministers of the Crown (Transfer of Functions).

20   'The King hath no prerogative, but that which the law of the land allows him'; see: the Case of Proclamations [1610] EWHC KB J22, 77 ER 1352.

21   British Broadcasting Corporation v Johns [1965] Ch 32 (CA).

22   R v Secretary of State for the Home Department, ex parte Northumbria Police Authority [1989] QB 26 (CA).

23   For example, the Bill of Rights 1689 put beyond doubt that there was no prerogative power to levy taxes.

24   Carltona Ltd v Commissioners of Works [1943] 2 All ER 560 (CA).

25   Cabinet Office, Ministerial Code, paragraph 1.2(b). An earlier version of the Code, expressing substantially the same principles, was endorsed by a Resolution of the House of Commons of 19 March 1997 CHC Deb 292 cols. 1046–1047.

26   Cabinet Office, Ministerial Code, paragraphs 1.1–1.2.

27   Ibid., Annex A.

28   Ibid., paragraph 7.25.

29   For guidance on establishing, managing, reviewing and abolishing arm's-length bodies, see:

www.cabinetofice.gov.uk/content/public-bodies-and-appointments.

30   Guidance on framework documents is published in HM Treasury Managing Public Money (2007), Chapter 7, Section 7.7.

31   Cabinet Office (2010) Machinery of Government Changes, p. 3.

32   Cabinet Office, Ministerial Code, paragraph 4.3.

Chapter Four

Government is a large and complex organisation and so it needs formal and informal mechanisms for discussing issues, building consensus, resolving disputes, taking decisions and monitoring progress. By convention, Cabinet and Cabinet committees take decisions which are binding on members of the Government. Cabinet and Cabinet committees are composed of government ministers, who are then accountable to Parliament for any collective decisions made. Collective responsibility allows ministers to express their views frankly in discussion, in the expectation that they can maintain a united front once a decision has been reached.

This chapter covers:

- principles of collective Cabinet government
- Cabinet
- political Cabinet
- Cabinet committees
- business of Cabinet and Cabinet committees
- procedures of Cabinet and Cabinet committees
- the Cabinet Secretariat
- the Cabinet Secretary

Collective Cabinet decision-making

Principles of collective Cabinet government

4.1   Cabinet is the ultimate decision-making body of government. The purpose of Cabinet and its committees is to provide a framework for ministers to consider and make collective decisions on policy issues. Cabinet and its committees are established by convention but it is a matter for the incumbent government to determine the specific arrangements for collective decision-making.

4.2   The Cabinet system of government is based on the principle of collective responsibility.[1]

All government ministers are bound by the collective decisions of Cabinet, save where it is explicitly set aside,[2] and carry joint responsibility for all the Government's policies and decisions.

4.3   In practice, this means that a decision of Cabinet or one of its committees is binding on all members of the Government, regardless of whether they were present when the decision was taken or their personal views. Before a decision is made, ministers are given the opportunity to debate the issue, with a view to reaching an agreed position. It is for the Prime Minister, as chair of Cabinet, or the relevant Cabinet committee chair to summarise what the collective decision is, and this is recorded in the minutes by the Cabinet Secretariat.

4.4   The Ministerial Code states: 'The principle of collective responsibility, save where it is explicitly set aside, requires that Ministers should be able to express their views frankly in the expectation that they can argue freely in private while maintaining a united front when decisions have been reached. This in turn requires that the privacy of opinions expressed in Cabinet and ministerial committees, including in correspondence, should be maintained.'[3] Chapter Eleven, paragraphs 11.18–11.20 provide more detail on the confidentiality of Cabinet papers and minutes and the application of the Freedom of Information Act 2000.

Cabinet

4.5 Cabinet is chaired by the Prime Minister, who also determines its membership.4 It will usually comprise senior ministers (see Chapter Three, paragraphs 3.9 and 3.10 on those ministers who are likely to be members of Cabinet). The Prime Minister may arrange for other ministers to attend Cabinet, either on a regular basis or for particular business (for example, the Attorney General to give legal advice). All members of Cabinet as Privy Counsellors are bound by the Privy Council Oath.5 The full list of Cabinet Members is available on the Cabinet Office website.6 31

4.6 Cabinet is established by convention and does not have specific terms of reference or powers laid down in legislation.

4.7 The Prime Minister determines and regulates the procedures of Cabinet, including when and where meetings take place. Cabinet currently meets in the Cabinet Room in 10 Downing Street every Tuesday morning while Parliament is sitting. Regional Cabinets can also take place, where the weekly Cabinet meeting is held in a location outside London. The agenda for Cabinet usually includes Parliamentary business, domestic and foreign affairs, and topical issues. The proceedings of Cabinet and Cabinet committees are recorded by the Cabinet Secretariat. The minutes produced are the official record of discussion and the decisions made. For more information, see paragraphs 4.34 and 4.35 on Cabinet minutes and paragraphs 4.51 and 4.52 on the Cabinet Secretariat.

Political Cabinet

4.8 At the discretion of the Prime Minister, members of Cabinet may meet to discuss party political matters in a 'political Cabinet'. Such meetings may take place in the Cabinet Room as usual, but they are not attended by officials and the conclusions of the discussion are not recorded in minutes.

Cabinet committees

Role of Cabinet committees

4.9 Cabinet committees help to ensure that government business is processed more effectively by relieving pressure on Cabinet. The committee structure also supports the principle of collective responsibility, ensuring that policy proposals receive thorough consideration without an issue having to be referred to the whole Cabinet. Cabinet committee decisions have the same authority as Cabinet decisions.

Structure of the Cabinet committee system

4.10 The Prime Minister decides – with the advice of the Cabinet Secretary – the overall structure of the Cabinet committee system, including the chair, deputy chair (if any),7 membership and the terms of reference of each Cabinet committee.8 Details are usually announced biannually in a written ministerial statement in Parliament.

4.11 Committees are usually established to consider a particular area of government business, such as home or domestic affairs, or national security. Where appropriate, sub-committees may be established to consider detailed issues and report as necessary to the full committee. Ad hoc or miscellaneous committees may also be established by the Prime Minister to carry out a particular task, usually over a limited timescale. For example, the National Security Council and its sub-committees were established in May 2010 and charged with overseeing and co-ordinating all aspects of Britain's security, including terrorism, other security threats, hazards, resilience, intelligence policy and the performance and resources of the security and intelligence agencies.

4.12 The committee structure varies depending on the requirements of the incumbent government. A list of the current committees, their terms of reference and the ministers who sit on them is available from the Cabinet Office website.9

National emergencies

4.13 The Cabinet Office Briefing Room (COBR) is the mechanism for agreeing the central government response to major emergencies which have international, national or multi-regional impact.10 Meetings at COBR are in effect Cabinet committee meetings, although there is no fixed membership, and they can meet at ministerial or official level depending on the issue under consideration. In general the chair will be taken by the secretary of state of the government department with lead responsibility for the particular issue being considered.11

Official committees

4.14 Official committees can be established to support Cabinet committees.12 Official committees are chaired by the Cabinet Secretariat. There is no fixed membership, but senior officials will be invited from each department with a minister who is a member of the relevant Cabinet committee.

4.15 Official committees may be convened for a variety of purposes, but would normally meet in advance of a Cabinet committee. This would enable them to consider the issues that would need to be covered in Cabinet committee papers and to help the Cabinet Secretariat identify points that are likely to be raised so that it can brief the chair of the Cabinet committee effectively.

Business of Cabinet and Cabinet committees

Issues for collective agreement

4.16 Collective agreement can be sought at a Cabinet or Cabinet committee meeting or through ministerial correspondence.

4.17 No definitive criteria can be given for issues which engage collective responsibility and the Cabinet Secretariat can advise where departments are unsure.13 At present, proposals will require consideration by a Cabinet committee if:

- The proposal takes forward or impacts on a Coalition agreement;

- The issue is likely to lead to significant public comment or criticism;

- The subject matter affects more than one department; and/or

- There is an unresolved conflict between departments.14

Issues for Cabinet

4.18 There are no set rules about the issues that should be considered by Cabinet itself and it is ultimately for the Prime Minister to decide the agenda, on the advice of the Cabinet Secretary. Cabinet and Cabinet committees can all take collective decisions and the level of committee at which a decision is taken should not be disclosed.15 However, the following is an indication of the kind of issues that would normally considered by Cabinet:

- Decisions to take military action;

- The Government's legislative priorities to be set out in the Queen's Speech;

- Issues of a constitutional nature, including matters relating to the monarchy, reform of

Parliament and changes to the devolution settlements;

- The most significant domestic policy issues;

- The most significant European or international business;

- issues that impact on every member of Cabinet; and

- National emergencies, including terrorism.

4.19 With the agreement of the Prime Minister, consideration of significant domestic or international policy issues may be taken by Cabinet at an early stage by way of a general discussion to inform the development of detailed policy by the relevant Secretary of State, or as a final step prior to announcement. Where an issue is brought to Cabinet at the end of the process, it would normally have been discussed and agreed by the relevant Cabinet committee.

Legislation

4.20 All legislative proposals relating to primary legislation require clearance from the Cabinet committee that is responsible for Parliamentary business and legislation, in addition to clearance through the relevant policy committee.16 Legislative proposals include public commitments to legislate within certain timescales, clearance of bills before introduction, amendments to bills during their passage through Parliament and the Government's position on Private Members' Bills.

4.21 The role of the Cabinet committee responsible for primary legislation differs from that of a policy Cabinet committee: it is concerned with the preparation and management of the legislative programme, rather than with agreeing government policy. The committee aims to ensure that the content of the legislative 33 The Cabinet Manual programme as a whole implements the Government's priorities, and that the passage of bills through Parliament can be successfully managed.

4.22 More information on clearing legislative proposals can be found on the Cabinet

Office website.17

Areas outside Cabinet collective decision-making

4.23 The Chancellor of the Exchequer's Budget and any other Budget statement are disclosed to Cabinet at a meeting on the morning of the day on which they are presented to the House of Commons, although the content of the proposal will often have been discussed with relevant ministers in advance of the meeting. The expectation is that the proposals will be accepted by Cabinet without amendment, although the Chancellor may, if necessary, make amendments.

4.24 Some ministerial posts have responsibility for quasi-judicial functions that are exercised by the individual minister and not through Cabinet. Examples of this are decisions on whether to grant planning permission following a call-in of planning applications, and whether to recommend exercise of the prerogative of mercy.

4.25 In a small number of cases, the Attorney General may write to relevant ministerial colleagues seeking any information that should be considered by a prosecuting authority when weighing the public interest in a prosecution.18This may happen, for example, where there is a risk that a prosecution may endanger national security, international relations or the safety of the Armed Forces abroad. This is known as a Shawcross exercise.19 However, the decision whether or not to prosecute remains a matter for the prosecuting authority.

Procedures of Cabinet and Cabinet committees

Agenda

4.26 An agenda is set for each Cabinet and Cabinet committee meeting. In the case of

Cabinet, items for the agenda are agreed by the Prime Minister. For other Cabinet committees, the agenda is agreed by the relevant chair.

4.27 Ministers may also give notice to the Cabinet Secretariat that they wish to raise business orally at a Cabinet or Cabinet committee and, where agreed, this is included as an item on the agenda.20

Papers and presentations

4.28 The Cabinet Secretariat is responsible for setting standards for the form and content of papers and presentations.21

4.29 For each agenda item, the lead minister, or ministers, will normally submit a paper for consideration by ministerial colleagues. However, any member of the committee and the Cabinet Secretariat can submit a paper on an agenda item, not just the lead minister.

4.30 Papers and presentations for Cabinet and Cabinet committees should include any information that is needed for ministers to make an informed decision. They should be concise and should set out the benefits, disadvantages and risks associated with the proposed policy. Any decisions that need to be made by ministers should be clear. Papers should explain any public expenditure implications. Where a paper does not reach the appropriate standard, the Cabinet Secretariat may refuse the paper, substitute their own note, or produce a cover sheet to the paper, highlighting the key issues for ministerial consideration.22

4.31 Final papers should be circulated the Friday before a Cabinet meeting and at least 48 hours before a Cabinet committee meeting. This ensures that the information can be properly considered by ministers before the item is discussed at Cabinet or the relevant Cabinet committee.

Clearance of proposals with expenditure or legal implications

4.32 Any proposals where other departments have an interest should be discussed with them before collective agreement is sought. Where proposals have public expenditure implications, the Treasury should be consulted before they are submitted for collective agreement.23

Where the department proposing the policy and the Treasury cannot agree in advance, any proposal for collective ministerial consideration should record the Treasury's position in terms which are acceptable to them. Policy proposals with public expenditure implications will not be agreed unless Treasury ministers are content. If necessary, issues can be referred to the Prime Minister or, if he or she so decides, to Cabinet for a decision.

4.33 Usually where critical decisions have legal implications they are considered after discussions with the Law Oficers.24 This includes issues that have the potential to lead to legal challenge or that might impact on the handling of government litigation.

Minutes

4.34 Minutes are taken for each Cabinet and Cabinet committee meeting, forming part of the historic record of government. They record the main points made in discussion and the Cabinet or Cabinet committee conclusions as summed up by the chair. To help preserve the principle of collective responsibility, most contributions by ministers are unattributed. However, points made by the minister introducing the item and the chair's summing-up are generally attributed.

4.35 It is the responsibility of the Cabinet Secretariat to write and circulate the minutes to members of Cabinet or the relevant Cabinet committee. This should be done within 24 hours of the meeting.

Minutes are not cleared with the chair of Cabinet or the Cabinet committee in advance of circulation. If a minister has a factual correction to make, the Cabinet Secretariat should be informed within 24 hours of circulation of the minutes.25

Attendance of ministers

4.36 The Ministerial Code states that Cabinet and Cabinet committee meetings take precedence over all other ministerial business apart from the Privy Council, although it is understood that ministers may sometimes have to be absent for reasons of Parliamentary business.26

4.37 Where a minister is unable to attend a Cabinet committee, with the consent of the chair, he or she may nominate a junior minister to attend instead. This will normally be another minister from the same department.27 However, attendance at Cabinet meetings cannot be delegated. Delegation may also not be allowed for certain Cabinet committee meetings, as determined by the Prime Minister.

4.38 Where the Prime Minister is unable to attend Cabinet, the next most senior minister should take the chair (following the order of precedence as determined by the Prime Minister). The same principle is adopted for Cabinet committees if the chair and any deputy chair are absent.

Attendance of officials

4.39 Attendance of officials (other than from the Cabinet Secretariat) at Cabinet and Cabinet committee meetings is kept to a minimum in order to allow ministers to have a free and frank discussion of the issues.

4.40 There is a standing invitation for a member of the Prime Minister's office to attend any Cabinet committee meeting, and the chair may be accompanied by a private secretary. This invitation also currently extends to the Deputy Prime Minister's office.

4.41 Where necessary, other officials may be invited to attend Cabinet committee meetings as set out in the terms of reference. Restrictions are in place regarding the attendance of other officials, and the Cabinet Secretariat must be consulted in advance should officials need to attend.

Quorum

4.42 There is no set quorum for Cabinet and Cabinet committee meetings. The decision to proceed with a meeting is made by the chair of the Cabinet committee, on the advice of the Cabinet Secretariat.

Implementation of decisions

4.43 Ministers are responsible for ensuring that their departments take whatever action is necessary to implement decisions made by Cabinet or Cabinet committees, and for reporting back to colleagues on progress if needed.

Cabinet committee correspondence

4.44 Most issues that require collective agreement do not need to be considered at a meeting of the relevant Cabinet committee and are handled through correspondence.28

4.45 Ministers seeking collective agreement should write to the chair of the relevant Cabinet committee or, exceptionally, to the Prime Minister as chair of Cabinet. The proposal to which ministers are being asked to agree should be clear from the letter, as should the date by when a response is requested (this should normally allow at least six working days).

4.46 Any replies should be addressed to the committee chair and all correspondence should be copied to the Prime Minister, the Deputy Prime Minister, members of the committee and the Cabinet Secretary. First Parliamentary Counsel should be copied in where a proposal has implications for the drafting of legislation.

4.47 Once all responses have been received from members of the Cabinet committee, the chair will (on advice from the Cabinet Secretariat) write to the minister confirming whether collective agreement has been reached or not, and setting out any conditions to that agreement.

4.48 If it is not possible to reach a decision in correspondence, the chair of the relevant Cabinet committee may decide to call a meeting to consider the issue.

The Devolved Administrations

4.49 Ministers should not copy Cabinet committee correspondence to the Devolved Administrations as they are separate administrations and not subject to the Government's collective responsibility. Consideration should be given to writing separately where they have an interest.29 Exceptionally, with the consent of the relevant chair, ministers from the Devolved Administrations may be invited to attend meetings. One such exception is Cabinet committee meetings which deal with an emergency response requiring input from both the Government and one or more of the Devolved Administrations.

4.50 Formal discussions of policy issues with the Devolved Administrations take place through the Joint Ministerial Committee (JMC).30

The Cabinet Secretariat

4.51 The Cabinet Secretariat exists to support the Prime Minister, and currently the Deputy Prime Minister, and the chairs of Cabinet committees in ensuring that government business is conducted in an effective and timely way and that proper collective consideration takes place. The Cabinet Secretariat is therefore non-departmental in function and consists of officials who are based in the Cabinet Office but drawn from across government.

4.52 The Cabinet Secretariat reports to the Prime Minister, the Deputy Prime Minister and other ministers who chair Cabinet committees.31 The Cabinet Secretariat prepares the agenda of Cabinet committee meetings, with the agreement of the chair; it also provides them with advice and support in their functions as chair; and it issues the minutes of the committees.

The Cabinet Secretary

4.53 The Cabinet Secretary is the head of the Cabinet Secretariat.32 The Cabinet Secretary is appointed by the Prime Minister on the advice of the retiring Cabinet Secretary and the First Civil Service Commissioner.

4.54 The Cabinet Secretary, unless unavoidably absent, attends all meetings of Cabinet and is responsible for the smooth running of Cabinet meetings and for preparing records of its discussions and decisions. This includes responsibility for advising the Prime Minister on all questions connected with the appointment and organisation of Cabinet committees, including membership and terms of reference.

Notes

1   Cabinet Office (2010) Ministerial Code, paragraph 2.3.

2   For example, HM Government (2010) The Coalition: our programme for government sets out a number of areas where collective agreement is explicitly set aside, for example, in relation to the referendum on the alternative vote, p. 27, and university funding, p. 32.

3   Cabinet Office, Ministerial Code, paragraph 2.1.

4   Ministerial selection may be subject to consultation in the event of a coalition government. See: Cabinet Office (2010) Coalition Agreement for Stability and Reform, paragraph 3.1.

5   A copy of the Oath can be found at: http://privycouncil.independent.gov.uk/wp-content/

uploads/2011/02/privy-counsellors-oath.doc.

6   www.cabinetofice.gov.uk/content/list-government-departments-and-ministers.

7   Under the Coalition Agreement for Stability and Reform, paragraph 3.5, each Cabinet committee has a deputy chair who is a member of the other political party to that of the chair. Both the chair and the deputy chair have the right to refer an unresolved issue to the Coalition Committee.

8   The Coalition Agreement for Stability and Reform, paragraph 3.1, states that the Prime Minister has agreed, and will continue to agree the establishment of Cabinet committees, appointment of members and determination of their terms of reference with the Deputy Prime Minister.

9   Cabinet Office (2010) Cabinet Committee System.

10   Cabinet Office (2010) Responding to Emergencies: The UK Central Government Response. Concept of Operations.

11   Cabinet Office, Cabinet Committee System, see: National Security Council (Threats, Resilience and Contingencies).

12   Cabinet Office (2010) Guide to Cabinet and Cabinet Committees, pp. 17–18.

13   Cabinet Office, Ministerial Code, paragraph 2.4.

14   Cabinet Office, Guide to Cabinet and Cabinet Committees, pp. 6–8.

15   Cabinet Office, Ministerial Code, paragraph 2.3.

16   Cabinet Office, Guide to Cabinet and Cabinet Committees, p. 10.

17   Cabinet Office (2011) Guide to Making Legislation.

18   Examples of prosecuting authorities are the Crown Prosecution Service, the Serious Fraud Office and the Public Prosecution Service (Northern Ireland).

19   In 1951 Sir Hartley Shawcross, who was the then Attorney General, provided a detailed explanation to the House of Commons of how prosecutors decide whether or not to prosecute and the role of the Attorney General. He also explained how the Attorney General may seek information from ministerial colleagues to inform prosecutorial decisions. See: Hansard, HC vol. 483, cols 679–90 (29 January 1951).

20   Cabinet Office, Guide to Cabinet and Cabinet Committees, p. 17.

21 Ibid., pp. 18–19.

22 Ibid., p. 19.

23 Ibid., p. 8.

24 Cabinet Office, Ministerial Code, paragraphs 2.10 and 2.12.

25 Cabinet Office, Guide to Cabinet and Cabinet Committees, p. 20.

26   Cabinet Office, Ministerial Code, paragraph 2.5.

27   A minister may, with the agreement of the chair, deputise to a member of the same party (see Cabinet Office, Guide to Cabinet and Cabinet Committees, p. 4).

28   Cabinet Office, Guide to Cabinet and Cabinet Committees, pp. 8 and 12–16.

29   Ibid., pp. 13–14.

30   Cabinet Office (2011) Devolution: Memorandum of Understanding and Supplementary Agreements, paragraphs 23–26.

31   Cabinet Office, Guide to Cabinet and Cabinet Committees, p. 5.

32   The offices of Cabinet Secretary and Head of the Home Civil Service are currently held by the same civil servant and have been since 1983. However, it was announced on 11 October 2011 that, from January 2012, those two posts will be held by two different civil servants.

Chapter Five

Parliament is central to the democracy of the United Kingdom. It is through Parliament that ministers are accountable to the people. The Ministerial Code makes clear that ministers have a duty to Parliament to account, and to be held to account, for the policies, decisions and actions of their departments and agencies; it is of paramount importance that ministers give accurate and truthful information to Parliament.

This chapter covers:

- The House of Commons and the House of Lords
- Core principles
- Government business
- Scrutiny of the Government
- legislation
- Public appointments
- The Parliamentary Commissioner for Administration
- The Comptroller and Auditor General and the National Audit Office.

The Executive and Parliament

The House of Commons and the House of Lords

5.1   Members of the House of Commons are directly elected by universal suffrage of the adult population. Most Members of the House of Lords are appointed for life by the Sovereign, on the advice of the Prime Minister. In addition, 92 hereditary peers are Members of the House (15 officeholders elected by the whole House, 75 Members elected by their party or group within the House, and the holders of the offices of Lord Great Chamberlain and Earl Marshal). The two archbishops, and 24 bishops, of the Church of England are also Members.

5.2   The House of Commons has primacy over the House of Lords. It is the democratically elected institution of the United Kingdom and the Government derives its democratic mandate from its command of the confidence of the Commons. The two Houses of Parliament acknowledge various conventions governing the relationship between them, including in relation to primacy of the House of Commons, financial privilege and the operation of the Salisbury-Addison convention.1

5.3   The House of Commons claims ancient rights and privileges over the House of

Lords in financial matters and, under the Parliament Acts 1911 and 1949, a Money Bill which has been passed by the House of Commons receives Royal Assent even if it has not been passed by the House of Lords. The final decision on what constitutes a Money Bill is made by the Speaker of the House of Commons, in accordance with the provision of the Parliament Act 1911.2

The financial powers of the House of Lords are also limited by the financial privilege of the House of Commons. The role of the House of Lords in relation to taxation and expenditure is to agree, not to initiate or amend. However, until the House of Commons invokes its financial privileges in respect of a particular piece of legislation, the House of Lords is free to act as it thinks it (unless an amendment is a prima facie material and intolerable infringement of privilege).3

5.4   Under the Parliament Acts, if the House of Lords rejects any bill passed by the House of Commons (other than a Money Bill or a bill containing any provision to extend the maximum duration of Parliament beyond five years) and the House of Commons passes an identical bill in the following session of Parliament and sends it to the House of Lords more than one month before the end of that session, then it receives Royal Assent without being passed by the House of Lords, unless the House of Commons directs to the contrary. For the purposes of the Acts, a bill is deemed to be rejected by the House of Lords if it is not passed by that House either without amendment or with such amendments only as may be agreed by both Houses. One year must elapse between the second reading of the bill in the first session and the bill being passed by the House of Commons in the second session. The bill must be passed the second time in an identical form to the one in which it was passed the first time, containing only such amendments that represent any amendments which have been made by the House of Lords in the former bill in the preceding session, or which are essential to allow for the passage of time.

The House of Commons may suggest further amendments to the House of Lords which, if the House of Lords agrees to them, are treated as if they were House of Lords amendments to which the House of Commons had agreed.4

5.5   Only the House of Commons can trigger an early general election by either passing a motion for an early general election, with the support of at least two-thirds of all MPs, or where there has been a vote of no confidence in the Government and 14 days have elapsed without the House of Commons passing a motion of confidence in the Government. The form for such motions is set out in the Fixed-term Parliaments Act 2011.5See Chapter Two for more on confidence.

Core principles

5.6   In all their dealings with Parliament, ministers should be governed by the following principles as set out in the Ministerial Code:6

•   Ministers have a duty to Parliament to account, and to be held to account, for the policies, decisions and actions of their departments and agencies.

- It is of paramount importance that ministers give accurate and truthful information to Parliament, correcting any inadvertent error at the earliest opportunity. Ministers who knowingly mislead Parliament will be expected to offer their resignation to the Prime Minister.

- Ministers should be as open as possible with Parliament and the public, refusing to provide information only when disclosure would not be in the public interest, which should be decided in accordance with relevant legislation, including the Freedom of Information Act 2000.

- Ministers should require civil servants who give evidence before Parliamentary committees on their behalf and under their direction to be as helpful as possible in providing accurate, truthful and full information in accordance with the duties and responsibilities of civil servants as set out in the Civil Service Code.

Government business

5.7 Government business takes precedence at most sittings of the House of Commons, with the exception of 60 days in each session which are allocated for opposition business, backbench business and Private Members' Bills.7 The subjects of debates in Westminster Hall are usually determined by backbenchers through a ballot system, and through the Liaison Committee8 and the Backbench Business Committee.9 This means that, in an average year, the Government has the equivalent of around 100 days at its disposal in the House of Commons.

5.8 In the House of Lords, the Government Chief Whip is responsible for the detailed arrangement of government business and the business of individual sittings. Government business is arranged by the Government Chief Whip through the 'usual channels'.10

5.9 The Leader of the House of Commons and the Leader of the House of Lords are government ministers. They work closely with the Government Chief Whip in each House to plan the Government's business. The Leader of the House of Lords has a responsibility to support the business of the House, and on occasion to make time available and to move the necessary motions for the House to dispose of certain internal or domestic business, even though it is not government business.11

5.10 The House of Commons Backbench Business Committee now has responsibility for scheduling some of the House's domestic business that was, before the 2010 Parliament, the responsibility of the Leader of the House of Commons. The Commons Leader is also an ex-oficio member of various statutory bodies related to the House of Commons, including the House of Commons Commission, the Public Accounts Commission, the Speaker's Committee for the Independent Parliamentary Standards Authority and the Speaker's Committee on the Electoral Commission.

Scrutiny of the Government

Parliamentary questions

5.11 Scrutiny of the Executive is one of the core functions of Parliament.

5.12 Members of both Houses can table questions – for oral or written answer – to ministers. In response to these, ministers are obliged to explain and account for the work, policy decisions and actions of their departments.12

5.13 Questions for oral answer in the House of Commons are tabled for answer by specific departments on specified days, according to a rota determined by the Government. In the House of Lords, up to four questions for oral answer may be taken each day, and may relate to the work of any department. Questions may be tabled for written answer to any department in either House on any sitting day. A written answer is sent to the Member tabling the question and is published in the Official Report of the relevant House. Additionally, the Speaker of either House may also allow for any urgent questions to be made at his or her discretion (see paragraph 5.16 on urgent questions in the House of Commons and private notice questions in the House of Lords).

Evidence to committees

5.14 Each House appoints select committees to scrutinise the work of government and hold it to account. In the House of Commons, a public bill committee may also take written and oral evidence on the bill that is before it.13 Ministers and civil servants usually appear before these committees to give evidence when they are invited to do so and supply written evidence when it is requested.14 Chapter Seven: Ministers and the Civil Service sets out in more detail how these rules apply to civil servants.

Statements to Parliament

5.15 When Parliament is in session the most important announcements of government policy should, in the first instance, be made to Parliament.15

5.16 Ministers may, subject to the relevant collective clearance being received, make statements to Parliament both orally and in writing on the work of their department. The Government, not the House of Commons or the House of Lords, decides whether or not a statement is made. A copy of the text of an oral statement is usually given to the Opposition shortly before it is made.16

Oral statements are followed by the relevant minister taking questions from Members on the issue. Ministers may also make written statements to each House. These are distributed through the Vote Office (House of Commons) and the Printed Paper Office (House of Lords) and published in Hansard the following day. When the Government does not plan to make a statement on a matter of public interest, the Speaker of the House of Commons may allow a Member to ask an urgent question on the subject, or less commonly to apply for an emergency debate17 to discuss the issue in more detail to ensure appropriate scrutiny. Private notice questions may be asked in the House of Lords and the decision over whether or not the question is of sufficient urgency to warrant immediate reply lies with the Lord Speaker.18

5.17 Announcements may also be accompanied by production of a paper presented to Parliament and published as a Command Paper.

Legislation19

Queen's Speech and introduction of legislation

5.18 Each session of Parliament begins with the ceremony of the State Opening, when the Sovereign formally opens Parliament. This includes the Queen's Speech, which outlines the forthcoming legislative programme. The Speech is written by the Government and approved by Cabinet, but delivered by the Sovereign from the throne in the House of Lords.

5.19 Following a State Opening, the Government's legislative programme is then debated by both Houses, usually for four or five days. In the debates, ministers explain and defend the proposed legislation of the Government. Topics for debate on each day are agreed by the usual channels.20

Passage of legislation

5.20 Every government bill goes through the following stages in each House.21 It is presented and read a first time; this is a formality which enables the bill to be published. The first substantive proceeding is the second reading, which is a debate on the principles of the bill. The debate is opened by a minister (normally the Secretary of State in the House of Commons). In the House of Commons the closing speech is usually given by another minister but the same minister frequently closes the debate in the House of Lords.

5.21 In the House of Commons, the committee stage of the bill is then usually dealt with by a public bill committee or sometimes by a committee of the whole House (see paragraph 5.22). The committee considers each clause of the bill in detail and may make amendments. Committee stage in the House of Commons is usually handled by a junior minister and the demands on the minister's time can be very significant, with a public bill committee typically meeting four times a week. Bills sent to a public bill committee in the House of Commons then return to the floor of the House, where they can be further amended on consideration (also known as Report stage). They then receive a final, third reading before being sent to the House of Lords. If either House amends the bill, then the other House only considers the amendments which were sent back, not the bill as a whole. This process may go through several iterations before agreement is reached between the two Houses.

5.22 Although the stages are the same in each House, there are three significant differences. In the House of Commons, proceedings on bills may be timetabled by means of a programme order.22 No equivalent procedure is currently used in the House of Lords. In the House of

Commons, bills are more usually committed to a public bill committee, which consists of a number of members specifically nominated to it and meets in a committee room away from the Chamber, whereas in the House of Lords bills are normally considered by a committee of the whole House (which meets in the Chamber) or a grand committee, which any peer may attend. However, bills with significant constitutional implications are in the House of Commons, by convention, taken in a committee of the whole House rather than in a public bill committee. The House of Lords also allows significant amendments to be tabled at third reading, whereas the House of Commons does not.

5.23 The Government has made commitments to Parliament about the supporting material which is to be provided in relation to each bill, much of which is contained in the Explanatory

Notes of the Cabinet Office Guide to Making Legislation.23 Draft bills, pre-legislative scrutiny and post legislative scrutiny

5.24 Ministers should consider publishing bills in draft for pre-legislative scrutiny, where it is appropriate to do so.24 Reports from the Commons Liaison Committee and the Lords Constitution Committee have identified this as good practice.25 Most draft bills are considered either by select committees in the House of Commons or by a joint committee of both Houses. The decision to establish a joint committee is formally taken by both Houses, on a proposal from the Leader of the House. Whether or not a joint committee is established, any committee of either House may choose to examine a draft bill. Once a committee has scrutinised and reported on the draft bill, the Government considers the committee's recommendations and may make alterations to the bill before it is formally introduced to Parliament. Pre-legislative scrutiny can help to improve the quality of legislation and to ensure that Parliament and the public are more involved with and aware of the Government's plans for legislation.

5.25 Once legislation has been passed, the Government has undertaken that ministers will (subject to some exceptions) publish a post-legislative scrutiny memorandum, within three to five years of Royal Assent.26 This includes a preliminary assessment of how the Act is working in practice, relative to its original objectives. The relevant select committee of the House of Commons may use the memorandum to decide whether or not to carry out a fuller post-legislative inquiry. Post-legislative scrutiny may also be conducted by Lords committees or a joint committee.27

5.26 Post-legislative scrutiny is in addition to other post-enactment review work, which might include internal policy reviews, but may be combined with reviews commissioned from external bodies, or post-implementation reviews as part of the Impact Assessment process, carried out by the department with responsibility for the Act.28

Secondary legislation

5.27 Many Acts of Parliament delegate to ministers powers to make more detailed legal provision. Several thousand Statutory Instruments – also known as delegated, or secondary, legislation – are made each year.29 Whether or not a piece of secondary legislation is subject to any Parliamentary procedure and, if so, what procedure it is subject to, is determined by the parent Act.

5.28 Much secondary legislation is made without being subject to any Parliamentary proceedings; it is simply approved and signed by the relevant minister. Under the negative Parliamentary procedure, an Instrument is laid before Parliament and does not require active approval but may be annulled by a Resolution of either House within 40 days of being laid. These Instruments are not routinely subject to debate in the House of Commons, but if a debate is granted then a minister will need to reply. In the House of Lords, negative instruments are debated fairly regularly.

Instruments subject to the affirmative Parliamentary procedure must be approved, usually by both Houses, before being made. They must therefore be subject to a debate in each House, although in the House of Commons this usually takes place in a committee.30 The minister will speak in the debate, whether in committee or on the floor of the House.

5.29 Acts can also delegate legislative power to persons other than ministers. For example,

Finance Acts sometimes delegate powers to make additional provision about taxation to the Commissioners for Her Majesty's Revenue and Customs. Other Acts delegate rule-making powers in particular areas, for example to Ofcom the communications regulator, or to committees in relation to procedural rules of courts or tribunals.

5.30 A power in an Act which enables primary legislation to be amended or repealed by secondary legislation (with or without further Parliamentary scrutiny) is often described as a 'Henry VIII power'. Questions as to whether it is appropriate for Parliament to confer particular Henry VIII powers, and questions as to the Parliamentary procedure appropriate for instruments made in the exercise of such powers, often arise during the passage of a bill. Such questions are a particular concern of the House of Lords Delegated Powers and Regulatory Reform Committee and Constitution Committee.31

The Budget and financial procedure

5.31 The Budget, which sets out the Government's taxation plans, is delivered by the Chancellor of the Exchequer, usually in March. Following his or her statement to the House of Commons, there is a four- or five-day debate, ending with votes on a series of motions to authorise the continuance of income tax and corporation tax, to impose any new taxes and increase the rates of any existing taxes, and to authorise any changes to tax law.

5.32 These motions, when passed, are known as the Budget Resolutions. The Resolutions determine the scope of the Finance Bill, which is formally introduced as soon as they are passed. The Finance Bill is then subject to the normal legislative process of the House of Commons, although committal is usually split between a public bill committee and a committee of the whole House. The House of Lords does not amend Finance Bills, but does debate them on second reading, with their subsequent stages being taken formally.32

5.33 All government expenditure must be authorised by Parliament.33 Ministers submit requests for expenditure to Parliament via the Treasury, in the form of Supply Estimates. The House of Commons approves these requests and the House of Lords' only function is to formally pass the bill that ratifies the approvals. The bill's consideration is a formality and proceedings on the bill are taken without debate in either House.

5.34 Parliament, through the National Audit Office (NAO) and the Committee of Public Accounts, monitors and audits government expenditure to ensure that it is consistent with what Parliament has authorised.

5.35 For more information on government finance and expenditure, see Chapter Ten.

Military action

5.36 Since the Second World War, the Government has notified the House of Commons of significant military action, either before or after the event, by means of a statement and has in some cases followed this with a debate on a motion for the adjournment of the House.34

5.37 In the two most recent examples of significant military action, in Iraq and Libya, Parliament has been given the opportunity for a substantive debate. Debates took place in Parliament shortly before military action in Iraq began in 2003. In relation to Libya, the Prime Minister made a statement in the House of Commons on 18 March 2011 in advance of military action, which was followed by a government motion for debate on 21 March, expressed in terms that the House 'supports Her Majesty's Government [...] in the taking of all necessary measures to protect civilians and civilian-populated areas'.35 5.38 In 2011, the Government acknowledged36 that a convention had developed in Parliament that before troops were committed the House of Commons should have an opportunity to debate the matter and said that it proposed to observe that convention except when there was an emergency and such action would not be appropriate.

Public appointments

5.39 Select committees of the House of Commons have a role in scrutinising certain key public appointments.37 Before such appointments are made, but after the selection process is complete, a pre-appointment hearing with the proposed appointee takes place in public. A report is then published setting out the committee's view on whether or not the candidate is suitable for the post. The views of the committee are almost invariably non-binding, but the Government has agreed that ministers should consider the committee's report before deciding whether or not to appoint the candidate.38

Pre-appointment hearings only apply to new appointments; however, select committees already take evidence from serving post-holders as part of their continuing scrutiny of public bodies and public appointments.39

The Parliamentary Commissioner for Administration

5.40 The Parliamentary Commissioner for Administration,40 known as the Parliamentary Ombudsman, is an officer of the House of Commons appointed by the Crown and is independent of the Government. In recognition of the Ombudsman's relationship with Parliament, the House now leads on the recruitment to the role. His or her powers and responsibilities are set out in the Parliamentary Commissioner Act 1967.

5.41 The Ombudsman investigates complaints that injustice has been caused by maladministration on the part of government departments or certain other public bodies. If the Ombudsman finds that there has been maladministration, the Government is not bound by the findings or recommendations, but if it rejects a finding it should have cogent reasons for doing so and it is potentially open to challenge if it unreasonably rejects a recommendation.41 In those cases where the Parliamentary Ombudsman makes a recommendation regarding the payment of compensation, departments follow the guidance set out in Managing Public Money. The Ombudsman's Principles outline the approach that public bodies should adopt when delivering good administration and customer service, and how to respond when things go wrong.

The Comptroller and Auditor General and the National Audit Office

5.42 The C&AG audits central government accounts on behalf of Parliament and reports on the value for money achieved by government projects and programmes. The audit and inspection rights are vested in the C&AG, who is an officer of the House of Commons, appointed by the Sovereign on an address proposed by the Prime Minister with the agreement of the Chairman of the Public Accounts Committee and approved by the House of Commons. Operating under the Budget Responsibility and National Audit Act 2011, the NAO is a corporate body with its own governance structure, constitution and functions, which include providing resources to the C&AG.42

5.43 The C&AG and the NAO have comprehensive statutory rights of access to the bodies to be audited.43 The NAO's budget is set by Parliament, not the Government, and oversight of the NAO is carried out by the Public Accounts Commission, which appoints the NAO's external auditors and scrutinises its performance.44

The NAO does not audit local government spending, publish statistical information or audit the spending of the Devolved Administrations in the rest of the UK.

Notes

1   Report of the Joint Committee on Conventions (2006) Conventions of the UK Parliament (HL265/HC1212). London: The Stationery Office.

2   Parliament Act 1911, s.1(2–3).

3   See: Jack M (ed.) (2011) Erskine May's Treatise on the Law, Privileges, Proceedings and Usage of Parliament, 24th edition. London: LexisNexis Butterworths, Chapter 36; and House of Lords (2010) Companion to the Standing Orders and Guide to the Proceedings of the House of Lords, 22nd edition. London: The Stationery Office, paragraphs 8.180 and 8.181.

4   Jack (ed.) Erskine May, pp. 648–651.

5   Fixed-Term Parliaments Act 2011, s.2(1).

6   Cabinet Office (2010) Ministerial Code, paragraph 1.2. An earlier version of the Code, expressing substantially the same principles, was endorsed by a Resolution of the House of Commons of 19 March 1997 (HC Deb 292 cols 1046–7).

7   House of Commons Standing Order 14.

8   The Liaison Committee considers general matters relating to the work of select committees; advises the House of Commons Commission on select committees; chooses select committee reports for debate in the House; and hears evidence from the Prime Minister on matters of public policy. The Liaison Committee is comprised of the chairs of other select committees. For more information on the Liaison Committee, see: www.parliament.uk/business/committees/ committees-archive/liaison-committee.

9   House of Commons Standing Order 10.

10   Companion to the Standing Orders and Guide to the Proceedings of the House of Lords, paragraph 3.30.

11   The role of the Leader of the House of Commons is described in more detail in Jack (ed.) Erskine May, p. 50. The role of the Leader of the House of Lords is described in more detail in the Companion to the Standing Orders and Guide to the Proceedings of the House of Lords, pp. 60–66.

12   For more details, see: Jack (ed.) Erskine May, pp. 352–368 and 503ff; and the Companion to the Standing Orders and Guide to the Proceedings of the House of Lords, pp. 92–104.

13   For a full list of select committees of both Houses, see: www.parliament.uk/business/committees.

14   Further guidance about the provision of information to select committees, known as the Osmotherly Rules, can be found in Cabinet Office (2005) Departmental Evidence and Response to Select Committees.

15   This principle was reaffirmed by a Resolution of the House of Commons on 20 July 2010 (HC Deb 514 c 244–288).

16   Cabinet Office, Ministerial Code, paragraph 9.5.

17   Jack (ed.) Erskine May, pp. 374–375.

18   Companion to the Standing Orders and Guide to the Proceedings of the House of Lords, paragraph 6.34.

19   Legislation is published in print by Her Majesty's Stationery Office and online at: www.legislation.gov.uk.

20   See: Jack (ed.) Erskine May, pp. 157ff.

21   For a fuller description of the primary legislative process, see: Jack (ed.) Erskine May, Chapters 26–29.

22   House of Commons Standing Orders 83A–83I.

23   Cabinet Office (2011) Guide to Making Legislation, s.B. For example, the Government has made a commitment to provide more detailed information on the human rights aspects of government bills in its explanatory notes (s.B, paragraph 10.62). Furthermore, it has also made it a requirement for copies of Impact Assessments to be placed in the House of Commons Vote Office as opposed to being deposited in the House of Commons Library (s.B, paragraph 13.7).

24   Ibid., paragraphs 22.1–22.33.

25   Notably in its annual reviews of the work of committees since 2001.

26   The undertaking was made in Post-legislative Scrutiny: the Government's Approach (Cm 7320). London: The Stationery Office, which sets out further details of how the process works.

27   Ibid., paragraph 9.

28   Further information on both pre- and post-legislative scrutiny can be found in Cabinet Office (2011) Guide to Making Legislation, s.20 and s.40.

29   The number of Statutory Instruments registered has exceeded 1,500 in each year since 1950 and has exceeded 2,000 in each year since 1984.

30   For a fuller description of the Parliamentary procedure relating to secondary legislation, see: Jack (ed.) Erskine May, Chapter 30. Some aspects of the procedure on Statutory Instruments are set out in the Statutory Instruments Act 1946.

31   House of Lords Delegated Powers and Regulatory Reform Committee (2009) Guidance for Departments on the Role and Requirements of the Committee requires that all Henry VIII powers in bills be clearly identified, and a full explanation given where the proposed Parliamentary procedure is not afirmative. The Constitution Committee routinely comments on the use of Henry VIII powers in bills; its findings are summarised in its annual reports to the House.

32   Companion to the Standing Orders and Guide to the Proceedings of the House of Lords, pp. 164–165.

33   HM Treasury (2011) Managing Public Money, Foreword and Chapter 1.

34   Examples before the Iraq debates of 2002 and 2003 include Afghanistan (4 and 8 October 2001); Kosovo (24 March 1999); and the Gulf War (17 and 21 January 1991).

35   The full text of the motion is at Hansard, HC cd. 700 (21 March 2011).

36   Leader of the House of Commons, Hansard HC col. 1066 (10 March 2011).

37   For more information, see: Liaison Committee (2010) The Work of Committees in 2008-09 (HC426). London: The Stationery Office, and subsequent Government responses published in 2010–11 (HC415 and HC564).

38   Exceptionally, the Budget Responsibility and National Audit Act 2011 requires the consent of the Treasury Select Committee to the appointment of the members of the Budget Responsibility Committee of the Office for Budget Responsibility.

39   Liaison Committee (2008) Pre-appointment Hearings by Select Committees: Government Response to the Committee's First Report of Session 2007–08 (HC594). London: The Stationery Office.

40   Further information on the Parliamentary Ombudsman and the Ombudsman's Principles can be found at: www.ombudsman.org.uk.

41   R (Bradley and others) v Secretary of State for Work and Pensions [2008] EWCA Civ 36.

42   More information on the NAO can be found at: www.nao.org.uk.

43   Government Resources and Accounts Act 2000, s.8; National Audit Act 1983, s.8.

44   National Audit Act 1983, s.2.

Chapter Six

Ministers are under an overarching duty to comply with the law.[1]

Ministerial decisions, and the process by which they exercise (or fail to exercise) their powers, can be reviewed by the High Court. The Law Officers are the chief legal advisers to the Government. The Lord Chancellor is responsible for ensuring an efficient and effective system for the administration of justice, while the judicial branch in each jurisdiction of the UK is headed by its own senior judge.

This chapter covers:

- The Law Officers
- Litigation involving ministers
- Legal advice and legal professional privilege
- Indemnity of legal costs
- The European Convention on Human Rights and the Human Rights Act 1998
- The Treasury Solicitor and the Government Legal Service
- Public inquiries
- Relations with the judiciary.

The Executive and the law

The Law Officers

6.1   The term 'the Law Officers'' refers to the UK Law Officers, who are the Attorney General, the Solicitor General and the Advocate General for Scotland. The Attorney General for England and Wales is also the ex-oficio Advocate General for Northern Ireland.2

6.2   The Attorney General is the Chief Law Officer for England and Wales and is the Chief Legal Adviser to the Crown. The Solicitor General is in practice the Attorney General's deputy and may exercise any function of the Attorney General.3

6.3   The Advocate General for Scotland is the principal legal adviser to the Government on Scots law. Jointly with the Attorney General, the Advocate General for Scotland also advises the Government on legal issues, including human rights and EU law.

The role of the Law Officers

6.4   The core function of the Law Officers is to advise on legal matters, helping ministers to act lawfully and in accordance with the rule of law. The Attorney General is also the minister with responsibility for superintending the Crown Prosecution Service and the Serious Fraud Office.

6.5   In addition to these roles, the Law Officers have a number of public interest functions. Acting in the public interest, independently of government, they may:

- refer unduly lenient sentences to the Court of Appeal;4

- bring contempt of court proceedings;5

- grant consent for some specific prosecutions;6

- intervene in certain charity7 and family law cases;8

- bring proceedings to restrain vexatious litigants;9

- appoint advocates to the Court;10 and

- refer points of law to the Court of Appeal after acquittals in criminal cases.11

Seeking Law Officer advice

6.6   The Law Officers must be consulted by ministers or their officials in good time before the Government is committed to critical decisions involving legal considerations.12 It has normally been considered appropriate to consult the Law Officers in cases where:

- The legal consequences of action by the Government might have important repercussions in the foreign, EU or domestic fields; 49

- A departmental legal adviser is in doubt concerning: – the legality or constitutional propriety of proposed primary or subordinate legislation which the Government proposes to introduce; – the powers necessary to make proposed subordinate legislation; or – the legality of proposed administrative action, particularly where that action might be subject to challenge in the courts;

- Ministers, or their officials, wish to have the advice of the Law Officers on questions involving legal considerations that are likely to come before Cabinet or a Cabinet committee;

- There is a particular legal difficulty (including one that arises in the context of litigation) that may raise sensitive policy issues; or

- Two or more government departments disagree on legal questions and wish to seek the view of the Law Officers.

6.7   The Law Officers have a role in ensuring the lawfulness and constitutional propriety of legislation. In particular, the Law Officers'' consent is required for legislative provisions that have a retrospective effect or where it is proposed that legislation is commenced within two months of Royal Assent. For more information on the Law Officers' and ministers' responsibilities regarding the European Convention on Human Rights (ECHR), see paragraphs 6.28–6.31 in this chapter.

6.8   Where advice from the Law Officers is included in correspondence between ministers, or in papers for Cabinet or ministerial committees, the conclusions of the advice may be summarised, if necessary. But if this is done, the complete text of the advice should be attached.13

6.9   The fact that the Law Officers have advised, or have not advised, and the content of their advice may not be disclosed outside government without their authority.14The Law Officers' advice to government is subject to legal professional privilege (LPP) and is confidential.

Litigation involving ministers

Judicial review

6.10 Ministers' decisions, and the process by which they exercise (or fail to exercise) their powers, can be reviewed by the High Court,15although the courts will usually hesitate to intervene in cases where they accept that, because of the subject matter (entering into treaties, the defence of the realm, the grant of honours, etc.), the decision-maker is better qualified than the courts to make a judgment.16

6.11 In judicial review the Court will consider a minister's exercise of public powers by reference to:

- legality (acting within the scope of any powers17 and for a proper purpose);18

- procedural fairness (for example, giving an individual affected by the decision the opportunity to be heard);19

- reasonableness or rationality (following a proper reasoning process to reach a reasonable conclusion);20 and compatibility (with the ECHR21 and EU law).22

6.12 Where a decision is one that the minister had discretion to make, the Court will examine it to decide whether logical or rational principles were applied when making it. If the Court finds that the decision was unreasonable, it will usually simply cancel (or 'quash') the decision, so requiring the minister to make a fresh decision that takes into account the guidance given by the Court.23

6.13 In practice, a minister will depend on civil servants in the decision-making process, and those officials will often be key witnesses in judicial review proceedings. Legally and constitutionally, however, the acts of officials are the acts of the ministers to whom they are accountable, and the Court will regard the minister as the person who is ultimately responsible for ensuring that a particular decision is made reasonably, fairly and according to law. See Chapter Three for more information on the powers of ministers and the Carltona principle.

Disclosure of documents

6.14 Disclosure as applied in private law litigation is not often used in judicial review. More often than not the Court accepts the facts as presented by the parties. This imposes a duty on all parties to be open and honest ('the duty of candour').24

6.15 The duty of candour weighs particularly heavily on ministers and civil servants, as they will have the information showing the basis for the decision under review and because they are representatives of the public interest, and it cannot be in the public interest for the Court to be presented with an incomplete or inaccurate account of the facts. While civil servants are responsible for finding the documents that relate to the matter in question, the lawyer acting for a minister in judicial review has overall responsibility for ensuring that the disclosure has been sufficient to discharge the duty of candour. Any matter of disclosure may be referred to the Attorney General if necessary.

6.16 Any minister who receives a notice or order to give evidence or produce Cabinet or departmental papers to a court should refer it to the Treasury Solicitor or departmental legal adviser. Where it is appropriate to do so, the Treasury Solicitor or departmental legal adviser may consult the Attorney General on the question of whether public interest immunity should be claimed. Any notice or order requiring the release of Cabinet or Cabinet committee papers should also be referred to the Cabinet Secretariat. (See Chapter Eleven on the protection of Cabinet and Cabinet committee papers.)

6.17 In judicial review proceedings it will usually be officials with relevant knowledge and responsibility within the department who give witness statements setting out the reasons for a minister's decision or action, although it may sometimes be desirable for a minister to give a statement. The Court will allow the cross-examination of a minister or official if it is necessary in order to enable the case to be disposed of fairly, but cross-examination is unlikely to be ordered if the chain of documents culminating in a decision is sufficiently complete and the witness statements address the matters raised in the case.

6.18 If there is any prospect of a minister becoming involved in legal proceedings in a personal capacity, or being a witness in proceedings in his or her personal capacity, he or she must consult the Law Officers in good time.25

Legal advice and legal professional privilege

6.19 LPP is a term that applies to the protection of confidential communications between a lawyer and a client. All legal advice that is provided to ministers or government agencies will attract LPP and should generally be protected from disclosure.

6.20 When the Crown engages in civil litigation it is generally in the same position concerning the disclosure of legal advice as any other litigator, but there are a limited number of situations in which the Government should apply wider considerations. Broadly speaking, the Government will generally waive LPP in any case where withholding the material in question might mislead either the opponent or the Court, particularly if the information is of central importance to the case and it is apparent that withholding the information would prevent the Court from reaching a conclusion that is fair and in the overall public interest.26

6.21 It is primarily for the department to which legal advice was given to decide whether to waive (or potentially waive) LPP. The department should consult its own legal advisers or the Treasury Solicitor's Department, and other departments where relevant. In cases of particular sensitivity, the matter may be referred to the Attorney General.

6.22 Where disclosure of legal advice is sought under the Freedom of Information Act 2000, section 42 provides an exemption for information which is subject to LPP, but it applies only if the public interest in withholding the information outweighs the public interest in disclosing it.27

Indemnity of legal costs

6.23 It is the practice for ministers to be indemnified by the Crown for any actions taken against them for things done or decisions made in the course of their ministerial duties.28 The indemnity will cover the cost of defending the proceedings, as well as any costs or damages awarded against the minister.

6.24 Ministers may be sued for acts which, although undertaken while a minister, have a more 'personal' aspect to them. For example, proceedings may be instituted alleging that a minister made a defamatory statement or that a minister has acted dishonestly or in bad faith. The extent to which a minister will be personally liable will depend on the law relating to the particular matter.

6.25 A minister may wish to bring proceedings in a personal capacity, for example where he or she believes that he or she has been defamed. Such proceedings may have a bearing on the minister's official position as well as on his or her private position. For example, he or she may require disclosure of official documents or evidence about things done in the minister's official capacity.

6.26 Decisions about whether public funds should meet a minister's costs in bringing or defending any such proceedings, or any damages awarded against a minister, are for the relevant accounting officer, who should be consulted about the matter at the earliest opportunity The accounting officer will wish to take into account any views of the Attorney General.

6.27 Where proceedings involving a minister are funded at public expense, it may be appropriate for any damages or costs awarded in a minister's favour to be paid to the Government. Again, such decisions are a matter for the relevant accounting officer.

The European Convention on Human Rights and the Human Rights Act 1998

6.28 The ECHR is divided into 59 Articles, which set out the substantive rights and freedoms and establish the European Court of Human Rights. A number of further substantive rights are set out in additional Protocols, of which the UK has ratified the First, Sixth and Thirteenth (the latter two together completely abolish the death penalty). Not all of the rights are absolute: many may be limited or interfered with in certain defined circumstances, so long as it is necessary and proportionate to do so. Each country is given a certain latitude in how it gives effect to the Convention rights in order to reflect national circumstances (the margin of appreciation).

6.29 The Human Rights Act 1998 gives further effect to the ECHR. The Act includes provisions that:

- make it unlawful for a public authority (which includes Ministers of the Crown in their official capacity), subject to certain limited exceptions, to act in a way that is incompatible with a Convention right.29 Domestic courts can provide certain remedies if a public authority does so;30 and

- require all courts and tribunals to interpret all legislation, as far as possible, in a way that is compatible with the Convention rights.31 The Act does not allow the courts to 'strike down' Acts of Parliament, thus respecting Parliamentary sovereignty. However, certain higher courts can indicate their view to Parliament that an Act of Parliament is incompatible with the Convention rights by means of a declaration of incompatibility, but it remains for the Government to make proposals to Parliament to change the law.

6.30 Under section 19 of the Human Rights Act 1998, the minister in charge of a government bill must, before second reading of the bill in Parliament, make a statement that in his or her view the bill's provisions are compatible with the Convention rights.32 Rarely, a minister may also make a statement that he or she cannot say that the bill's provisions are compatible but that the Government nevertheless wishes Parliament to proceed with the bill.33

6.31 Before a bill is introduced or published in draft, ministers must submit to the Cabinet committee responsible for legislation the ECHR memorandum which sets out the impact, if any, of the bill on the ECHR rights. The memorandum must be cleared by the Law Officers before it is submitted to the committee, and so should be sent to the Law Officers at least two weeks before being circulated to committee members.34

The Treasury Solicitor and the Government Legal Service

6.32 The Treasury Solicitor's Department is a non-ministerial department responsible to the Attorney General. It provides legal services to more than 180 central government departments and other publicly funded bodies in England and Wales.

6.33 The Treasury Solicitor is the Head of the Government Legal Service, which joins together around 2,000 government lawyers who work across some 30 government organisations. Other organisationally separate areas of government legal provision, such as the Crown Prosecution

Service, the Foreign and Commonwealth Office and the Office of the Parliamentary Counsel, maintain close links with the Government Legal Service, as do the legal teams supporting the Devolved Administrations.

Public inquiries

6.34 The Government has statutory and non-statutory powers to call inquiries. Statutory public inquiries are governed principally by the Inquiries Act 2005. It provides that a minister may establish an inquiry if it appears to him or her that particular events have caused or are capable of causing public concern, or if there is public concern that particular event may have occurred.35

The Act provides how the inquiry should be set up and conducted and how its findings should be reported. It grants powers compelling the attendance of witnesses and the production of documents, and provides for the conduct of an inquiry to take place in private if necessary.

6.35 A non-statutory inquiry may be held where, for example, all relevant parties have agreed to co-operate, and it may be convened and concluded more quickly – and perhaps more cheaply. The terms of reference will normally be determined by the relevant minister in discussion with officials.

6.36 The Prime Minister must be consulted in good time about any proposal to set up a major public inquiry.36 The relevant Scottish ministers must be consulted about proposals to set up inquiries on matters relating to Scotland which are not reserved under the Scotland Act 1998. There are similar requirements relating to Wales and Northern Ireland.37 The power to hold an inquiry should be used sparingly and consideration given to potential costs.

Relations with the judiciary

The Lord Chancellor and the judiciary

6.37 The principles underpinning the separation of powers between the Executive and the judiciary are set out in the Constitutional Reform Act 2005. The Act provides for a system based on concurrence and consultation between the Lord Chancellor and the Lord Chief Justice, while clarifying their respective constitutional roles. The Lord Chief Justice is head of the judiciary in England and Wales, Head of Criminal Justice and President of the Courts of England and Wales.38

6.38 There is a duty to uphold the continued independence of the judiciary extending to the Lord Chancellor, Ministers of the Crown and 'all with responsibility for matters relating to the judiciary or otherwise to the administration of justice',39 including civil servants and members of Parliament. There is also a duty not to seek to influence judicial decision-making through special access; for example, individual cases should not be discussed between ministers and judges.

6.39 The Lord Chancellor has special responsibility to defend judicial independence and to consider the public interest in respect of matters relating to the judiciary.40 The Lord

Chancellor also has a responsibility to ensure that there is an efficient and effective system for the administration of justice. The Lord Chancellor is under a general duty to provide sufficient resources to support the business of the courts in England and Wales.

6.40 The Lord Chief Justice may make written representations to Parliament on matters which he or she believes are of importance relating to the judiciary or the administration of justice. In practice, dialogue between the judiciary and ministers occurs through consultation and regular meetings. Judges may comment on the practical effect of legislative proposals insofar as such proposals affect the operation of the courts or the administration of justice. However, principles of judicial independence mean that the judiciary should not be asked to comment on the merits of proposed government policy, and individual judicial ofice-holders should not be asked to comment on matters that may then require the judge to disqualify him or herself in subsequent litigation.

Supreme Court of the UK

6.41 The Supreme Court of the UK has taken over the appellate jurisdiction of the House of Lords[41] as the final court of appeal for all civil law cases in the UK and for all criminal law cases in England, Wales and Northern Ireland. The Supreme Court hears appeals on arguable points of law of general public importance, and concentrates on cases of the greatest public and constitutional importance. The impact of Supreme Court decisions extends beyond the parties involved in any given case and plays an important role in the development of UK civil law and criminal law in England, Wales and Northern Ireland. The Court also hears cases on devolution matters under the Scotland Act 1998, the Government of Wales Act 2006 and the Northern Ireland Act 1998.

Notes

1 Cabinet Office (2010) Ministerial Code, paragraph 1.2.

2 The equivalent offices in the Devolved Administrations are the Lord Advocate in Scotland, assisted by the Solicitor General for Scotland; the Attorney General for Northern Ireland (the Chief Legal Adviser to the Northern Ireland Executive); and the Counsel General to the Welsh Government (who is the General Counsel to the Welsh Government).

3 Law Oficers Act 1997, s.1(1).

4 Criminal Justice Act 1988, ss.35 and 36.

5 Contempt of Court Act 1981, s.7.

6 For example, offences under the Explosive Substances Act 1883; the Terrorism Act 2000; Part III of the Public Order Act 1986; the Law Reform (Year and a Day Rule) Act 1996; and section 128 of the Serious Organised Crime and Police Act 2005.

7 The Attorney General has a number of powers in relation to charity cases arising from his or her role as parens patriae.

8 Family Law Act 1986, s.59.

9 Senior Courts Act 1981, s.42.

10 See Memorandum from the Lord Chief Justice and Attorney General published at paragraph 39.8.1 of the Civil Procedure Rules.

11 Criminal Justice Act 1972, s.36.

12 Cabinet Ofice (2010) Ministerial Code, paragraph 2.10.

13 Ibid., paragraph 2.12.

14 Ibid., paragraph 2.13.

15 Supreme Court Act 1981, s.31; and Part 54 of the Civil Procedure Rules.

16 For example, see Home Secretary v Rehman [2001] 3 WLR 877.

17 The exercise of statutory powers conferred on particular ministers is usually subject to collective agreement. For more information, see Chapter Three, paragraph 3.30.

18 These irst three grounds of review were referred to as 'illegality', 'procedural impropriety' and 'irrationality' by Lord Diplock in Council of Civil Service Unions v Minister for the Civil Service [1985] AC 374 at 410.

19 Ibid.

20 Ibid.

21 Human Rights Act 1998, s.1(2).

22   European Communities Act 1972, s.2(1).

23   For example, see R v Secretary of State for the Environment, ex parte Nottinghamshire CC [1986] AC 240.

24   For further details on the duty of candour, see: Treasury Solicitor's Office (2010) Guidance on Discharging the Duty of Candour and Disclosure in Judicial Review Proceedings.

25   Cabinet Ofice, Ministerial Code, paragraphs 7.16–7.17.

26 For example, see: R v Secretary of State for Transport, ex parte Factortame Ltd and others [1999] UKHL 44.

27   For more details, see: www.justice.gov.uk/guidance/freedom-and-rights/ freedom-of-information/foi-assumptions-legal. htm and www.justice.gov.uk/guidance/docs/ foi-exemption-section42.pdf.

28   References to ministers in this section also apply to former ministers, including those of previous governments.

29   Human Rights Act 1998, s.6.

30   Ibid., s.4 and s.8.

31   Ibid., s.3.

32   Ibid., s.19(1)(A).

33   Ibid., s.19(1)(B).

34   Cabinet Ofice (2010) Guide to Making Legislation, paragraph 11.8.

35   Inquiries Act 2005, s.1.

36   Cabinet Ofice, Ministerial Code, paragraph 4.10.

37   Inquiries Act 2005, s.27.

38   The Lord President of the Court of Session is the head of the judiciary in Scotland. The Lord President has authority over any court established under Scots Law. The Lord Chief Justice of Northern Ireland is the head of the judiciary in Northern Ireland. More information is available at:

www.judiciary.gov.uk.

39   Constitutional Reform Act 2005, s.3(1).

40   Ministry of Justice (2011) Her Majesty's Courts and

Tribunals Service: Framework Document, s.1.2.

41   Constitutional Reform Act 2005, Part III, s.40, Schedule 9. 5

Chapter Seven

The Civil Service supports the government of the day to develop and implement its policies, and in delivering public services. Civil servants are required to carry out their role in accordance with the values set out in the Civil Service Code and the Constitutional Reform and Governance Act 2010.

Central to this is the requirement for political impartiality. Civil servants must act solely according to the merits of the case, and serve governments of different political parties equally well.1

This chapter covers:
- the Civil Service
- the role of ministers and officials
- the Civil Service Code
- the role of permanent secretaries
- the role of special advisers
- civil servants' evidence to Parliamentary select committees
- public appointments.

Ministers and the Civil Service

The Civil Service

7.1   Civil servants are servants of the Crown. The Civil Service supports the government of the day in developing and implementing its policies, and in delivering public services.2 Civil servants are accountable to ministers, who in turn are accountable to Parliament.3

The role of ministers and officials

7.2   Ministers are required to uphold the political impartiality of the Civil Service and not ask civil servants to act in any way that would conflict with the Civil Service Code or the requirements of the Constitutional Reform and Governance Act 2010.4 Ministers also have a duty to give fair consideration and due weight to informed and impartial advice from civil servants, as well as to other considerations and advice in reaching policy decisions.5

7.3   In addition, civil servants should not be asked to engage in activities likely to call into question their political impartiality or give rise to the criticism that resources paid from public funds are being used for party political purposes.6

The Civil Service Code

7.4   Civil servants serve the elected government of the day,7 in line with the standards set out in the Civil Service Code. The Code sets out the standards of conduct and behaviour expected of all civil servants in upholding the core Civil Service values, and in carrying out their duties and responsibilities, and makes clear what they can and cannot do.8 The core Civil Service values and standards of behaviour as set out in the Code are:

•   <u>integrity</u> – putting the obligations of public service above your own personal interests;

•   <u>honesty</u> – being truthful and open;

- objectivity – basing your advice and decisions on rigorous analysis of the evidence; and

- impartiality, including political impartiality – acting solely according to the merits of the case and serving equally well governments of different political persuasions.

7.5 The Code also makes clear that civil servants must not misuse their official position or information acquired in the course of their official duties to further their private interests or those of others. Where an actual or perceived conflict of interest arises between a civil servant's official duties and responsibilities and their private interests, they must make a declaration to senior management so that senior management can determine how best to proceed.

7.6 The Code also sets out the procedure that civil servants should follow if they believe that they are being required to act in a way that conflicts with the Code, or if they have concerns about a possible breach of the Code.9 This includes raising the matter with line management, or with departmentally nominated officers who have been appointed to advise staff on the Code. It also includes the option to take the matter directly to the independent Civil Service Commissioners. The Public Interest Disclosure Act 1998, which protects individuals who make certain disclosures of information in the public interest, may apply.

7.7 The Constitutional Reform and Governance Act 2010 provides the statutory framework for the Civil Service by providing a power for the Minister for the Civil Service (the Prime Minister) to manage the Civil Service, and making provision for a code of conduct for civil servants which specifically requires them to carry out their duties in accordance with the core Civil Service values set out above.10

The Act also provides for recruitment to the Civil Service to be on merit on the basis of fair and open competition, and provides for a statutory Civil Service Commission to safeguard and oversee the application of this fundamental principle, and to investigate complaints under the Civil Service Code.11

7.8 **The role of permanent secretaries**

7.9 The most senior civil servant in a department is the permanent secretary. Each permanent secretary supports the government minister who heads the department and who is accountable to Parliament for the department's actions and performance. In a limited number of departments there may be more than one permanent secretary, or a deputy or second permanent secretary to deal with issues of operational or national significance, such as national security. Permanent secretaries are responsible to the Cabinet Secretary or the Head of the Civil Service for the effective day-to-day management of the relevant department, or the particular issues for which they are responsible (for more information on the Cabinet Secretary, see Chapter Four, paragraphs 4.53 and 4.54).

7.10 The permanent secretary is normally the accounting officer for their department, with a personal responsibility to report directly to Parliament for the management and organisation of the department.

The role of special advisers

7.11 Special advisers are employed as temporary civil servants to help ministers on matters where the work of government and the work of the party, or parties, of government overlap and where it would be inappropriate for permanent civil servants to become involved. They are an additional resource for the minister, providing assistance from a standpoint that is more politically committed and politically aware than would be available to a minister from the permanent Civil Service.12 Limits on the number of special advisers that ministers may appoint are set out in the Ministerial Code.13

7.12 The employment of special advisers adds a political dimension to the advice and assistance available to ministers, while reinforcing the political impartiality of the permanent Civil Service by distinguishing the source of political advice and support.14

7.13 The Code of Conduct for Special Advisers sets out the kind of work special advisers may do if their minister wants it, and their relationship with the permanent Civil Service, including that special advisers must not ask civil servants to do anything that is inconsistent with their obligations under the Civil Service Code, or exercise any powers in relation to the management of any part of the Civil Service 15

Civil servants' evidence to Parliamentary select committees

7.14 Parliamentary select committees have a crucial role in ensuring the full accountability of the Executive to Parliament. Ministers are expected to observe the principle that civil servant who give evidence before Parliamentary select committees on their behalf and under their direction should be as helpful as possible in providing accurate, truthful and full information in accordance with the duties and responsibilities of civil servants as set out in the Civil Service Code.16

7.15 Detailed guidance to officials who may be called upon to give evidence to Parliamentary select committees is contained in the Cabinet Office memorandum Departmental Evidence and Response to Select Committees, commonly called the Osmotherly Rules (July 2005).

7.16 The memorandum summarises conventions that have developed in the relationship between Parliament, in the form of its select committees, and successive governments. Parliament has generally recognised these conventions, but the memorandum is a government document and therefore has no Parliamentary standing or approval.

7.17 Public appointments

7.18 A public appointment is an appointment to the board of a public body or to an office. This includes non-executive appointments to the boards of non-departmental public bodies and non-ministerial departments as well as non-executive appointments to the boards of NHS trusts and other NHS bodies. Public appointees of this kind are not employees but office-holders. Most public appointments are made by ministers.17 For more on Parliamentary scrutiny in relation to some public appointments, see Chapter Five.

7.19 Many public appointment processes are regulated by the independent Commissioner for Public Appointments who is appointed under the Public Appointments Order in Council 2002. The Commissioner publishes a Code of Practice setting out the process for making public appointments, which are made on merit.18

7.20 Ministers are ultimately responsible for the appointments they make and will have involvement in some way in the process. For example, they may be consulted at the planning stage of the appointments process and will approve the skills and experience needed for the post. They may also be consulted throughout the process and will make the final decision on which candidate to appoint.

7.21 The role of individual public appointees will vary but, in general, those appointed to the board of a public body have collective responsibility for the overall performance and success of the body in question. Their role is to provide strategic leadership, direction, support and guidance. The Cabinet Office provides general guidance on the role of non-executive board members.19 The specific responsibilities of individual public appointees should be set out in letters of appointment and in related documents.

7.22 All public appointees are expected to work to the highest personal and professional standards. To this end, codes of conduct are in place for boards of public bodies and all public appointees. Along with others in public life, they are expected to follow the Seven Principles of Public Life: selflessness, integrity, objectivity, accountability, openness, honesty and leadership.

Notes

1 Cabinet Office (2010) Civil Service Code, paragraph 3.

2 Civil servants in the Scottish Government and the Welsh Government are part of the Home Civil Service and report ultimately to the Head of the Civil Service, the Cabinet Secretary. Civil servants in the Northern Ireland Executive are not part of the Home Civil Service but are part of the Northern Ireland Civil Service.

3 See: Cabinet Office (2010) Ministerial Code, Cabinet Office, Civil Service Code and the Constitutional Reform and Governance Act 2010.

4 Cabinet Office, Ministerial Code, paragraph 5.1.

5 Ibid., paragraph 5.2.

6 Cabinet Office, Ministerial Code, paragraphs 14–15.

7 Some civil servants are accountable to the ofice-holder in charge of their organisation.

8 Civil servants working for the Scottish Government and the Welsh Government and their agencies have their own versions of the Code. Similar codes apply to the Northern Ireland Civil Service and the Diplomatic Service. Civil servants working in non-ministerial departments in England, Scotland and Wales are covered by the Code.

9 Cabinet Office, Civil Service Code, paragraphs 16–18.

10 Constitutional Reform and Governance Act 2010, ss.3–5.

11 Ibid., ss.10–11.

12 Paragraph 2 of the Code of Conduct for Special Advisers (Cabinet Office, 2010) makes clear that special advisers are appointed to serve the Government as a whole, not just their appointing minister.

13 Cabinet Office, Ministerial Code, paragraph 3.2.

14 The Constitutional Reform and Governance Act 2010 provides for the appointment of special advisers as temporary civil servants (s.15), and for the publication of a code of conduct which must specify restrictions on special advisers' activities (s.8).

15 Further information on the role of special advisers can be found in Cabinet Office (2010) Code of Conduct for Special Advisers.

16 There is an exception for accounting officers as set out in Cabinet Office (2005) Departmental Evidence and Response to Select Committees, paragraph 5.

17 Ministerial appointments to the majority of NHS bodies are delegated to the Appointments Commission.

18 The Commissioner for Public Appointments' Code of Practice can be found at: www.publicappointmentscommissioner.independent.gov.uk/codeofpractice/index.html.

19 Cabinet Office (2011) Code of Practice for Board Members of Public Bodies.

Chapter Eight

The establishment of the directly elected Scottish Parliament, National Assembly for Wales and Northern Ireland Assembly has had a significant impact on the governance of the UK. In addition, central government has devolved powers and responsibilities to local authorities, which are directly elected and have limited power to tax.

This chapter covers:

- devolution
- Parliament and legislation
- Scotland
- Wales
- Northern Ireland
- relations with the Devolved Administrations
- funding of devolution
- local government in England.

Relations with the Devolved Administrations and local government

Devolution

8.1 The main legislative basis for devolution in Scotland, Wales and Northern Ireland is set out in the Scotland Act 1998, the Government of Wales Act 2006 (which largely superseded the Government of Wales Act 1998) and the Northern Ireland Act 1998. Each of the devolution settlements is different but features of all three settlements are as follows:

• Parliament remains sovereign: it expressly retains the power to legislate on any matter, whether or not the devolved legislature could legislate in that area, and to amend the powers of the devolved legislatures (although see paragraph 6.41).

• The devolved legislatures may amend Acts of Parliament (insofar as they relate to devolved responsibilities). However, they may not amend certain entrenched1 or protected2 enactments (for example the Human Rights Act 1998, most provisions of the devolution Acts and the European Communities Act 1972).

• The devolved legislatures and administrations may only legislate or act in relation to the part of the UK for which they are responsible.

• The devolved legislatures and administrations must legislate or act in a way that is compatible with EU law and the European Convention on Human Rights.

• The devolved legislatures can pass legislation that is within the respective competence of that legislature. The Supreme Court has jurisdiction to hear disputes where it is alleged that a devolved legislature or administration has exceeded its powers.3 The UK or devolved Law Officers may raise challenges on this basis, as may individuals. (See Chapter Six for more information on the Supreme Court and the Law Officers.)

8.2   Broadly speaking,4 legislation provides that government ministers and Parliament remain responsible, among other things, for:

- the constitution;

- international relations and defence;

- national security;

- nationality and immigration;

- macroeconomic and fiscal policy;

- broadcasting;

- the UK tax system (except for the Scottish variable rate of income tax in Scotland); and

- social security (which is transferred in Northern Ireland, although there is a principle of parity with the system in Great Britain).

8.3   Broadly speaking,5 legislation provides that government ministers and Parliament are not responsible for the following areas in 63 Scotland, Wales and Northern Ireland, as they have been devolved to the respective legislatures and administrations:

- health and social care;

- education and training;

- local government;

- housing;

- transport;

- agriculture, forestry and fisheries;

- the environment and planning;

- tourism, sport and heritage; and

- economic development.

8.4 Responsibility for policing and justice is also devolved in Scotland and Northern Ireland.

Parliament and legislation

8.5 Parliament remains sovereign and retains authority to legislate on any issue, whether devolved or not. It is ultimately for Parliament to decide what use to make of that power. However, the Government proceeds in accordance with the convention that Parliament would not normally legislate with regard to devolved matters except with the agreement of the devolved legislature. The Devolved Administrations are responsible for seeking such agreement as may be required for this purpose on an approach from the UK government.6

In practice this agreement is signaled by a devolved legislature passing a Legislative Consent Motion. Details of the procedures for such motions are set out on the websites of the three legislatures.7

Scotland

8.6 Following a referendum in Scotland in 1997, the 1998 settlement established a devolved legislature (the Scottish Parliament) and administration (the Scottish Executive, now referred to as the Scottish Government) in Scotland. The Scottish Parliament is composed of 129 members elected either on a constituency basis or on a regional list basis.

8.7 The Scotland Act 1998 identifies a number of issues that are reserved (Schedule 5 to the Act). These are issues on which the Scottish Parliament is not able to legislate. Any other areas not listed in Schedule 5 to the Scotland Act are devolved. The Scottish Government's powers largely follow the legislative competence of the Scottish Parliament. This means that, where an area is devolved, the Scottish ministers will also exercise functions in that area.

8.8 The Scotland Act 1998 also allows the Scottish Parliament to vary the basic rate of income tax by three pence in the pound, following which funding allocated to the Scottish Government would be amended to reflect the reduced or increased tax yield. This power has not been used to date. The Scotland Bill introduced in the UK Parliament on 30 November 2010 will, if enacted, increase the financial accountability of the Scottish Parliament and revise the boundaries of the devolution settlement.

Wales

8.9 Following a referendum in Wales in 1997, the Government of Wales Act 1998 established the National Assembly for Wales as a corporate body. The Welsh Assembly is currently composed of 60 members elected either on a constituency or a regional list basis.

8.10 The Welsh settlement was revised by the Government of Wales Act 2006. That Act dissolved the corporate body and formally established an executive, the Welsh Assembly Government (now referred to as the Welsh Government), which exercises executive functions, and a legislature to pass laws equivalent to Acts of Parliament within its areas of legislative competence.

8.11 The 2006 Act also created a mechanism for granting law-making powers on an incremental basis to the National Assembly for Wales, either in Acts of Parliament or Orders in Council conferring legislative competence (Legislative Competence Orders). The mechanism for the National Assembly for Wales to obtain broader primary law-making powers was also set out in the 2006 Act, in the event of a 'yes' vote in a referendum. A referendum was held on 3 March 2011 which resulted in a vote in favour of enhanced law-making powers for the National Assembly. These powers came into force on 5 May 2011.

8.12 Unlike the Scottish and Northern Ireland settlements, the Welsh settlement operates on a 'transfer' model, whereby those areas not specifically transferred to the Assembly under Schedule 7 to the 2006 Act remain the responsibility of the Government and Parliament.

Northern Ireland

8.13 The 1998 Belfast Multi-Party Agreement and Northern Ireland Act 1998 form the basis of the constitutional structure in Northern Ireland. The Northern Ireland Assembly is composed of 108 members elected by single transferable vote on the basis of multi-member constituencies.

8.14 The Northern Ireland Executive is an inclusive power-sharing Executive chaired by a First and deputy First Minister who hold office jointly. It has 11 departmental ministers, 10 of whom are selected according to their party strengths in the Assembly by the d'Hondt process. The appointment of the Minister for Justice takes place on the basis of cross-community support.

8.15 The Northern Ireland devolution settlement, provided for in the Northern Ireland Act 1998, apportions matters into three categories of legislative competence:

- Excepted matters (listed at Schedule 2 to the 1998 Act) are those on which the Assembly cannot legislate unless the matter is ancillary to a reserved or transferred matter. These matters therefore generally remain for Parliament.

- Reserved matters (listed at Schedule 3 to the 1998 Act) are those on which the Northern Ireland Assembly can legislate but only with the consent of the Secretary of State and subject to Parliamentary control.

- Transferred matters (anything not listed at Schedules 2 or 3) comprise everything else upon which the Northern Ireland Assembly is free to legislate.

8.16 Ministerial functions in relation to transferred matters in Northern Ireland generally lie with Northern Ireland ministers and departments. These broadly replicate the legislative competence of the Assembly, although the Executive does not have the power to act on reserved matters.

Relations with the Devolved Administrations

8.17 Relations between the Government and the Devolved Administrations are underpinned by a Memorandum of Understanding between the four administrations, which is supported by Devolution Guidance Notes that set out advice on working-level arrangements.8 These are not legally binding, but are designed to set out principles to which all officials can adhere. Many departments also have bilateral concordats with the Devolved Administrations, dealing with areas of shared interest and setting out a framework for co-operation.9

8.18 The foundation of the relationship between the Government and the Devolved Administrations is mutual respect and recognition of the responsibilities set out in the devolution settlements.

8.19 The Secretaries of State for Scotland, Wales and Northern Ireland represent the interests of Scotland, Wales and Northern Ireland in the Government, and promote the Government's objectives in Scotland, Wales and Northern Ireland. The Scotland Office, Wales Office and Northern Ireland Office manage the day-to-day devolution issues which arise between the Government and the Devolved Administrations and are responsible for managing the devolution settlements. Additionally, the Secretary of State for Northern Ireland has responsibility for matters relating to national security in Northern Ireland.

8.20 Inter-governmental relations are conducted through formal mechanisms, such as the Joint Ministerial Committee (JMC) and the British–Irish Council (BIC), and working-level bilateral relationships across policy areas.

Joint Ministerial Committee

8.21 The JMC is established under the Memorandum of Understanding between the Government and the Devolved Administrations.10 It is chaired by the Prime Minister or his or her representative. The Secretaries of State for Scotland, Wales and Northern Ireland also attend this meeting along with the leaders of the Devolved Administrations. Other ministers are invited to attend as appropriate when issues relevant to their areas of responsibility are to be discussed. The JMC has two sub-committees:

- JMC (Domestic) which deals with domestic matters of mutual interest and is currently chaired by the Deputy Prime Minister; and

- JMC (Europe) which discusses EU issues, including the Government's priorities for meetings of the European Council, and which is currently chaired by the Foreign Secretary

8.22 The JMC also oversees a formal mechanism for resolving disputes under a protocol to the Memorandum of Understanding.11

8.23 There is also a finance ministers' quadrilateral, which considers financial and economic matters, and which takes place alongside the JMC.12 Additionally, government ministers regularly interact directly with ministers of the Devolved Administrations. Doing so helps to ensure good communication with the Devolved Administrations where the Government's activities have some bearing on their responsibilities or where all four administrations can benefit from working together on matters of mutual interest.13 The JMC is supported by a joint secretariat of staff from the Cabinet Office and the Devolved Administrations.

The British–Irish Council

8.24 The Devolved Administrations and the Crown Dependencies participate in the BIC, along with the governments of the UK and the Republic of Ireland. The BIC was established under the multi-party agreement reached in Belfast on Good Friday 1998 in order to 'promote the harmonious and mutually beneficial development of the totality of relationships among the people of these islands'.1 It proceeds by consensus, and all member administrations are equal partners of the BIC. A Joint Secretariat is currently provided by the UK and Irish governments. A Standing Secretariat is due to be established in Edinburgh.

8.25 Summit meetings of the BIC for heads of administration (or a nominated representative) are held twice a year, and include relevant ministerial representation in line with the chosen sectoral theme for each summit. Each member administration is expected to host, and therefore chair, a summit in turn. The lead government minister represents the UK's interests at summit meetings, including on key strategic decisions for the Council. Other sectoral ministerial meetings occur more frequently and only involve ministers who are responsible for the particular subject.

Funding of devolution

8.26 Government funding for the Devolved Administrations is normally determined within spending reviews in accordance with policies set out in the Statement of Funding Policy.15

The Devolved Administrations receive their funding largely from a government block grant, although the Scottish Parliament may affect the size of the Scottish block grant by exercising its tax-varying powers. Changes to the level of funding for the Devolved Administrations are determined by the Barnett formula, which compares departmental allocations within government with devolved responsibilities and population share to ensure that comparable changes in public spending are the same per capita. Additional allocations or reductions in the budgets of government departments in a spending review will therefore have further repercussions for the funding of the Devolved Administrations and the Exchequer given that funding for the Devolved Administrations is calculated in addition to what is made available to departments. A Devolved Administration is free to spend its allocation according to its own priorities in devolved areas, as agreed by the relevant devolved legislature. The Government places no conditions on expenditure of the Devolved Administrations.

Local government in England

8.27 Local authorities are statutory bodies created by Acts of Parliament.16 They are not accountable to Parliament, as they are directly elected by their local communities. However, ministers can direct local government to adhere to national policy frameworks where legislation permits. The current approach to, and structure of, local government in England is compliant with the European Charter of Local Self-Government.17

8.28 Local government is a devolved responsibility in Scotland, Wales and Northern Ireland.

8.29 In England, there is both single-tier and two-tier local government:

- <u>Single tier:</u> in the major metropolitan conurbations, including London, in a number of the larger towns and cities and in some shire county areas, there is single-tier local government, although London additionally has a strategic regional authority (the Greater London Authority). In these areas, responsibility for most local government services rests with a single authority.

- <u>Two tier:</u> this is where some local services are provided by a county council and others by a district council. The county council provides large-scale services across the whole of the county and is responsible for the more strategic issues, such as strategic planning, refuse disposal, libraries and personal social services. The district council has a more local focus, with responsibility for providing services in its own area, such as environmental health, housing and refuse collection.

8.30 Parish and community councils also operate at the grassroots level in many areas.
Central government funding of local government in England

8.31 Local authorities are responsible for their own finances within centrally set parameters and budgets. However, the Government sets the overall level of central government funding for local government in England, and decides expenditure priorities and standards for improvement. Some funding will, exceptionally, be ring fenced for particular activities. The level of funding may vary from year to year to reflect changes in responsibilities placed on local authorities by government.

8.32 There are three main areas of local authority spending. These are:

- <u>capital expenditure,</u> for example on roads or school buildings;

- <u>revenue</u> spending on council housing; and

- <u>revenue expenditure,</u> mainly on pay and other costs of running services other than council housing. While, in the main, local authorities cannot use capital funding to meet revenue expenditure, they are able to spend revenue funding on capital projects.

8.33 Local authorities may borrow additional funds for capital expenditure, but not for revenue expenditure. This can be done without government consent, provided they can afford to service the debt from their own resources. They also have the power to raise Council Tax – a local tax on domestic property set by local authorities. Councils can choose whether to charge Council Tax and at what level (subject to the Government's reserve powers to cap excessive increases, which are subject to Parliamentary approval).18

Local authorities also raise a significant amount through fees and charges, some of which are set centrally and others by local authorities themselves. Most are limited to cost recovery.

Notes

1	Northern Ireland Act 1998, s.7.

2	Scotland Act 1998, Schedule 4, Part I, ss.1–6, Government of Wales Act 2006, Schedule 5, Part II, s.3.

3	For further information on the Supreme Court, see: www.supremecourt.gov.uk/about/the-supreme-court.html.

4	Settlements differ and the details should therefore be checked in each case.

5	Ibid.

6	Cabinet Ofice (2011) Devolution: Memorandum of Understanding and Supplementary Agreements.

7	Ibid., Part I, paragraph 14.

8	For more information, see: www.cabinetofice.gov.uk/content/devolution-united-kingdom.

9	The aim and purpose of concordats is to preserve existing good working relationships and ensure that the business of government is conducted smoothly and efficiently under devolution. Their purpose is not to create legal obligations or restrictions on any party; rather, they will set the ground rules for administrative co-operation and exchange of information. For further information, see: Ministry of Justice (2009) Devolution Guidance Note 1, Annex. For examples of bilateral concordats, see: http://archive.defra.gov.uk/corporate/about/with/ devolve/index.htm.

10	The terms under which the Joint Ministerial Committee operates can be found in Devolution: Memorandum of Understanding, Part I, paragraph 24.

11	Ibid.

12	Ibid., Part II, A3.7.

13	Ibid., Part I, paragraph 4.

14	The Agreement, 1998, strand 3.

15	HM Treasury (2010) Funding the Scottish Parliament, National Assembly for Wales and Northern Ireland Assembly: Statement of Funding Policy.

16	Historically, boroughs were created by Royal Charter, reformed by successive legislation such as the Municipal Corporations Act 1835, Local Government Act 1972, through to the Local Government and Public Involvement in Health Act 2007.

17	European Charter of Local Self-Government 1985.

18	The current Council Tax system was established by the Local Government Finance Act 1992, with Council Tax capping powers for central government being introduced by the Local Government Act 1999.